From Entrepreneur to Big Fish

7 Principles to *Wild* Success

From Entrepreneur to Big Fish

7 Principles to *Wild* Success

Lorin D. Beller

Big Fish Publishing

Lorin Beller - From Entrepreneur to Big Fish

Big Fish Publishing

Big Fish Publishing
85 Bentwood Court
Albany, NY 12203
www.bigfishnation.com

ISBN: 0-97-695580-6

Library of Congress Control Number: 2005905308

Printed in the United States of America
First Printing 2005

Cover Design: Linda Demers
Editor: RaeAnne Marsh

From Entrepreneur to Big Fish:
7 Principles for Wild Success
Early Endorsements

"Going from entrepreneur to big fish takes new thoughts, new behaviors, a shift in the way you think. This book will help you think in different ways so you'll get different results -- like becoming the great Big Fish."

Michael Losier
Author of best-seller:
Law of Attraction: The Science of Attracting More of What You Want and Less of What You Don't

"Lorin Beller has a gift of bringing out the 'Big Fish' in everyone."

Steve Mitten
President of the International Coaches Federation and Master Certified Coach, British Columbia

"Inspirational, passionate, exciting, reflective, thought-provoking; and it honors those who truly wish to play a bigger game of life!"

Samy Chong
Chief Inspirational Officer of Corporate Philosopher Inc.

"I highly recommend this book to all entrepreneurs and business executives. The lessons discussed are simple but so very important. If we all used these simple lessons, the world would look different. More people would be smiling and commenting on how wonderful is the weather rather than complaining about how hard they work and how they are not appreciated. I finally understand what it means to 'Love yourself first.' It used to seem selfish; now it seems so simple. Why didn't I understand?"

Robin Barros
Owner of Barrels Boxes & More
Flying Fish in the Big Fish Nation Program

"*From Entrepreneur to Big Fish* was everything and more than I expected. It's an easy read, practical guide for *'Wild Success'* that goes with the flow! I've followed the *7 Big Fish Principles* for the past three years and, thanks to Lorin Beller's coaching and swimming with *The Big Fish*, I now host my own daily radio talk show and have recently acquired a weekly spot on a nationally syndicated show. The 7 Principles have truly guided me, a *50-Plus Baby Boomer*, in the direction of my vision. 'To truly change your world, you cannot let the world change you.' 'Choose your attitude and your actions and then boldly act.'"

Kathryn Zox
The Kathryn Zox Show
WSDE AM1190 Cobleskill/Albany, NY

"Lorin Beller is inspirational... In her *Big Fish Nation* business and book, Ms. Beller provides principles for enjoying life, loving life each day... principles and skills that can benefit everyone: business people, parents, youth, etc. Key to understanding the principles are applying them via practice, practice, practice. Having a personal coach or significant other to help us stay focused to realize our purpose and passion to serve others can truly lead to joy and success."

Dave Troy
Retired Principal

"Lorin Beller's book, *Seven Principles for Wild Success*, draws together all of the elements of being successful into a practical, down-to-earth guide for living life. Her book is a structure for refining your dreams, simplifying the roadmap to getting there and making the journey enjoyable. In applying her principles, I have recognized huge improvements in my personal and professional life. It is an indispensable map of how to live my life fully."

Paul Magliaro
Senior Vice President and Wealth Advisor
Morgan Stanley

"This book challenges each of us to take a different path. It is not a cookie cutter formula that can be implemented in two days. Big Fish are on a journey that never ends, a journey to make their lives better, to make the lives of people around them better and to make the world a better place to live. In *From Entrepreneur to Big Fish*, Lorin has provided a field guide for our journeys not only as entrepreneurs but as people."

Danny Wheeler
Entrepreneur and Big Fish

"Lorin is contagious. She has tapped into the essence of living. She lives in the zone that people have been searching for throughout the ages. Let her infuse you with this river of life through her book, *From Entrepreneur to Big Fish.*"

L.A. Reding
Master Certified Coach

"As a producer/director, I've always wanted to work on global issues on an international level. During this year as a participant in Big Fish Nation I took the big leap and filmed in 3 countries in Africa and also obtained credentials to film Kofi Annan speaking at the UN. Being a Big Fish means not waiting for the invitation; it means writing the invitation yourself. Lorin knows how to help you find the courage and direction to do just that. Lorin's wisdom is captured in this book."

Amy Hart
Filmmaker and Big Fish (Great White Shark)

"Thank you for giving a book to the world that helps us strengthen our belief in what can be."

Alison R. Brown
President, ALMEC International, Author, Educator

"Every entrepreneur needs to read this book; Lorin discusses the true essence of the entrepreneur - creating success as defined by each person. For me that was stepping into my power, following my heart, and believing in myself while being supported by other wonderful Big Fish. She also challenges us to think BIG and plan where we want our dream to go, and provides us with measurable steps to get there. All the while not letting fear or any other obstacles deter us from our dream."

Kelly Lipfert
Owner of Urban Details and Big Fish (Dolphin)

"The ongoing prosperity of the United States will depend on its ability to continue to innovate and create the advancements in every business sector that will keep it competitive in the global marketplace. *From Entrepreneur to Big Fish* outlines an inspirational, self-reflection process that can contribute to the achievement of that goal on personal and professional levels. Its use with young people, tomorrow's business and social leaders, can fill the gaps of connection with the emerging generation and their social and academic environments."

Niel Tebbano
Director of Operations
Project Lead the Way

"*From Entrepreneur to Big Fish: 7 Principles to Wild Success* is a valuable guide to living the life you really want."

Rieva Lesonsky,
Editorial Director
Entrepreneur Magazine

"I have read quite a few management and leadership texts, but this without a doubt is a gem of a book that will expand the power of all the 'Big Fish' and those with 'Big Fish' aspirations."

Douglas D. Barone
Chief of Staff to Chairman of the Board and CEO
MetLife, Inc.

"One in nine baby boomers will live to be 100 years old. Millions will live beyond their 80th birthday. It would a shame if only a few reached their full potential. Lorin Beller is bubbling with energy and advice for those who want it. If you open yourself up to her wisdom and guidance, you can do more and be happier with the life you live. May it a long one!

Edie Werner,
Futurist, and President of
Weiner, Edrich, Brown, Inc.

"This book is fluid and flows easily from one point to the next. I feel so much energy in the words, and it motivates me to follow through in my own life, to really take action!"

Susan Sikule
Doctor of Veterinary Medicine,
Owner, Just Cats
Big Fish (Dolphin)

"When I first heard of Big Fish Nation and Lorin Beller, I intuitively knew she was on to something. What I did not know at the time is that Big Fish Nation would transform my life. I am more grounded, have a vision and a plan, taking bold action and more conscious of the power of my thoughts and words than ever before."

Frankie Boyer
The Frankie Boyer Show
Big Fish (Dolphin)

"The Big Fish Principles, if followed by a corporate sales team, will enable the team be more effective as a whole. The individuals will be more successful for themselves and the company, and have more fun along the way."

Robert Blake
District Sales Manager
ResMed Corporation

To My Parents.

Carol Beller: You have the most tender heart and soul of any person I know and have always supported me from your heart. You have taught me to listen to mine and live fully from it. My life is rich because of you.

Jeff Beller: You have great vision and incredible determination. Watching you have impact in the world through my life gives me hope that we can do anything we set our minds to. Because of you, I believe in me.

In love and gratitude to both of you.

Table of Contents

Prologue

We all know that moment when we realize we want more from our life. We want it to slow down or we want it to be "bigger," or we want more time or we want more passion, or we want to be happier or to be in charge of it... We want something! And we know that there is more. We ask the question, "*What is this thing called life really all about*?"

I remember the day someone referred to me as a 'Big Fish.' It was a new boyfriend's friend. He said to my new boyfriend, "You caught the Big Fish." My boyfriend's response was, "No, *she* caught the Big Fish." I realized at that moment... *We all want to be Big Fish!*

However, it is not about who thinks we are a big fish; what matters most is if *we* think we are Big Fish. This is when transition begins to happen. This is when we begin to step into our full lives; this is when we begin to feel like we are fully living; and this is when we are truly serving people like we want to be impacting the world. And this is also when life becomes easy.

The purpose of this book is to inspire entrepreneurs and those who want to be *entrepreneurs of their lives* to make a decision to begin to swim like a Big Fish; to see themselves like the Big Fish, and see that they have the full potential of becoming one – not in years, not next month, but today, right now! It is that magical moment when we look in the mirror for the first time in our lives and see our possibilities and our potential. It is that magical moment when we walk around in the world with our shoulders back and our eyes fully open, ready to embrace life. It is that magic moment when we say, "Yes!" to our full potential that has been living in us all along but now we know it is there and we are excited about the possibilities.

This book will outline 7 principles to *wild* success. Which happens first: Do you read the principles and then become a Big Fish, or do you decide to become a Big Fish and then read the principles? Just like the chicken and the egg… the answer does not matter – it matters more that you "*swim on*" as a Big Fish!

From a bigger perspective, becoming a Big Fish is about living fully, having less fear, taking action – bold action – in spite of fears, going for your big life – whatever that might be to you. Being a Big Fish is about feeling more, loving more, having the little things in life become the big things, being more awake in your life spiritually and having more success at the same time because you are taking full responsibility for your life as a Big Fish.

So many people never get to this place. So many people think that in order to get to this "special place" or do something special they have to have some big tragedy in their life. I want to dispel this myth. Although I am the author of this book, I am like the girl next door. I have not had any big terrible tragedy happen (thank God!) and I have had a pretty "normal" life thus far. I grew up with two parents, who divorced when I was a teenager; I graduated from high school, just missing high honors; and I went to a state college. I had a job out of college as a counselor and was let go because of lack of funding. I created a few businesses at which I failed at and also one that was quite successful. I have been married and divorced. You see, a pretty typically life. I am the typical "girl next door," and if I can be a Big Fish, so can you!

I am a Big Fish. I know that what I set my mind to, I can create. I also know that life is perfect just the way it is. I do not regret any part of my life; I see each aspect of it as a needed part to help create who I am today. I have a successful business development program and I have grand goals for this company. I look forward to seeing more of the world. It is my intention to love each day of my life. I want to cry tears of joy often. I am committed to my work and I love to play in this world and experience the magic of the basics like sunsets, oceans, wild animals, laughter, snow on my face and thunder bolts, too.

So, the intention of this book is to create more, a lot more, Big Fish in the nation and in the world; to create a community of Big Fish that are of like mind, that have grand visions, yet love life and take full responsibility for creating those grand visions. ***Wanna be a Big Fish?***

Introduction

Before we get started, let's be clear on what an **entrepreneur** is. Webster defines entrepreneur as *"one who organizes, manages, and assumes the risks of a business or enterprise."* If we look at what an **enterprise** is, Webster says it is *"a project or undertaking that is especially difficult, complicated, or risky"* and *"readiness to engage in daring action."* That being said, aren't we all entrepreneurs of our own life? ***Let's dive in!***

What is a Big Fish?

Let us start with the end – the goal or the vision of what a Big Fish is. A big fish is an awakened entrepreneur who is wildly successful *and* has a lifestyle that creates room to live life, too. A Big Fish always attracts more Big Fish, self-actualizing people.

Big Fish are people who are in charge of their life. They insist on learning from every experience. They also insist on living fully in each moment. Big Fish speak from their hearts rather than only from their heads. They have grand visions for how their business or work will impact the world. Their visions are grand and realistic to them. Others may not agree or see reality in their vision, but that does not matter to a Big Fish. Big Fish have a *written* plan to back up that big vision. Big Fish are awake in life. They pay attention to what they are giving energy to in each thought, word and action, and at the same time are free in their thoughts. Big Fish are happy. They are happy around people and they are happy alone. They know and trust that there is a bigger, divine plan that they are co-creating with the world. They set a clear intention and stay awake to how the world works with that intention, or not. Big Fish are constantly striving to be their true best. Big Fish walk their talk; you will not see Big Fish tell someone what to do without practicing it themselves. If they feel something is important, they will follow through rather than just talk about it. Big Fish are direct and insist on real conversation even if it is hard and challenging. Big Fish know that real and honest communication is the tool to deep and meaningful relationships. Big Fish only want to be in deep and meaningful relationships, whether that is with clients, vendors, employees, friends, family, significant other or the store clerk who is checking them out at that moment. You will find Big Fish saying things to strangers that leave that person inspired in thought or opened up to a whole new way of thinking about their life. Big Fish can be found doing the "crazy" thing now and then…

In other words, Big Fish live fully. If they have a sense of wanting to try something new, they do it. You will not find them wishing or hoping; you will find them doing and taking charge of what they want, and, at the same time, being relaxed and not forcing anything. Big Fish live in the paradox of setting clear intention and letting go of that goal yet still being responsible for it. Big Fish also live in a paradox of full responsibility and full freedom to create the full life they know they can live. Big Fish have fun. They have fun at work, they have fun at home, they have fun stuck in traffic and they have fun on the water.

Every single person in the world has the potential to be a Big Fish. As a matter of fact, when more do choose to step into being a Big Fish, we will have a more peaceful world and we will see more happy people in our world. In the moment when a person decides they are going to be in integrity with themselves, it is in that moment he or she becomes a Big Fish.

Some think that becoming a Big Fish takes years of practice and training, but that is simply not the case. It does take years to constantly improve ourselves, learn and grow. But it takes only an instant to *decide* that you are going to live in your own truth and be aware of thoughts, actions and words and how they affect you and the world around you each moment. It is when we are committed to living a life that is aligned with who we want to truly be in the world and the impact we want to have that we become a Big Fish. Big Fish are true to themselves first and foremost.

In this moment, you get to decide: Are you a Big Fish? Or, more importantly, **are you ready to be a Big Fish**? *Are you ready?*

Before we dive in, let's be clear on what being a Big Fish is really about. It is about *change*. It is about *letting go* of the old way of doing business and living life. There is the old adage that my friend and colleague, Larry Bjurstrom, used to share in our stress management programs:

If you always do what you have always done, you will always get what you have always gotten.

Being a Big Fish is about working smarter, not harder, as the old cliché goes. This book will truly answer the question of *how* to work smarter, not harder. Being a Big Fish is about *doing things differently* and *receiving different results; wild results!* – results that you have only been dreaming about. Being a Big Fish is about integrating the inner work (self-awareness and self-reflection) with the outer work (actions, words, goals and objectives) so that there is alignment between the two. Being a Big Fish is about being in integrity with ourselves. In the process of becoming a Big Fish, you will learn all about yourself, your brilliant amazing self, and all that comes with that!

Practical tips and a writing exercise:

Now that you know what being a Big Fish is, what is it that you know you need to *let go* of in order to move in this direction? Let's be even clearer and more specific. What 10 things is it time to let go of or leave behind in order to step into being your Big Fish? These can be physical items or, emotionally, there may be beliefs or ways you are doing things that are getting in your way. You decide. We all have things that we need to let go of, to clean up so to speak, and streamline. This list can be updated at any time as you are reading the book. Keep adding to it. Be conscious of what you want to get rid of. We are more nimble and go with the flow when we are carrying less "stuff" with us.

1. ____

2. ____

3. ____

4. ____

5. ____

6. ____

7. ____

8. ____

9. ____

10. ____

Now, do what ever it takes to eliminate the above items from your life! Take action today.

ONE

Give Energy to That Which You Want to Grow.

This sentence is small but powerful. It is the basic principle on which all the rest are based. In every single moment, you get to decide – what are you giving energy to? What Big Fish know is that giving energy to something actually creates more of the same.

What, really, is energy? Energy is our thoughts. Energy is our spoken word. Energy is also how we spend our time. Energy is our written word. Our listening to someone else's spoken word gives energy to those words in addition to the energy given to them by the person speaking the words. So, what we listen to, we are giving energy to. Our behaviors are also energy. Therefore, we need to become really aware of what we are truly giving our energy to. This is the first critical step in taking your life and business to a higher level. Notice what you are giving energy to. Notice. Notice. Notice. It all starts here.

Joseph Campbell talks about this concept in a way that helps us train ourselves to know what we are giving energy to. He says we should follow the energy – the higher energy. If in business we are feeling heavy and sluggish, that is a great awareness to stop what we are doing and either consciously change our energy or delegate this task to someone else who has higher energy around it. The person with the most energy around a task is going to do it best most of the time.

In corporate America, we use the word “resources” for people, money, time, etc. These are simply various forms of energy. So we can also look at energy from this perspective, and ask, “What are we putting our resources toward?” If we put resources toward something, we are giving it energy.

A story about this kind of choice came to me from a stranger. I was in church around Thanksgiving time. The minister asked if anyone wanted to share what they were grateful for, and many people did so. One man’s story inspired me and reminded me that we all can find something to give our energy to that will have better impact on us and our world around us. He was a scruffy guy, large in stature. His arm was in a sling of some sort and he was dressed in a flannel shirt and jeans. He said he was thankful for the pain in his shoulder because the pain reminded him of the car accident he had been in a few weeks before where he almost lost his life – it reminded him that he is alive and that it is time to live fully. That man is a true Big Fish. He was giving energy to gratitude and to life through his words and thoughts, and because of that, I imagine, he felt better more quickly and healed faster.

Another story is about a friend of mine whom I have known for years. She is in her early 50s and has been working at a technical job most of her life. Recently, she has become much more aware of her thoughts and actions, and is waking up to the fact that she creates her life; no one else does it for her. She was telling me that she was practicing meditation for the first time in her life and she was meditating on 'wanting a certain person back in her life.' But she was missing a small yet significant part of the Big Fish process: Give energy to that which you want to grow or that which you want more of. If she is giving energy to "wanting" and "longing" and "emptiness" in hoping for this person to come back, guess what she is creating: More of the same! More of the wanting and the longing and the hoping, not the fullness of being in a fulfilling relationship.

If we want to create more of something, like a fulfilling relationship, we have to find where that *already exists* in our life in this moment – even if it is in a small, tiny way – and then give energy to that, be grateful for that! This may be a very fine line but it makes all the difference in the world in whether our energy is working for us or against us.

So in each moment, you get to decide what you are giving energy to. If the feeling of that energy is high, you are attracting more high-energy "stuff" to you in that moment; if you are feeling low, you are attracting lower energy stuff. You get to make the choice about what you are putting out into the world each moment. You are fully responsible for your own experiences.

Byron Katie says, *"The world is nothing but my perception of it. I see only through myself. I hear only through the filter of my story."*

This is true in the business world as well. Years ago, when I worked in a corporate setting, what I found is that much of the chat among team leaders was about what was not working in the organization. That organization crumbled very quickly. I find that, in most corporate settings, "water cooler" talk does not give energy to what we want more of. Yet water cooler talk has energy!

This principle of energy is based on the concept that like attracts like. We attract partners who are like us. We attract friends who are like us. We attract customers who are like us. We attract employees who are like us. Whatever it is we want to grow, that is what we need to give energy to. When we express in ourselves – our thoughts as well as our actions – the kind of person we want to attract, we create an energy that will grow and attract more of that same kind of energy.

This is the reason Big Fish attract more Big Fish. And these like-minded Big Fish manifest great things and achievements quickly because of their like-mindedness. In other words, when Big Fish give energy to possibility in the world and their life, they attract others who are doing the same.

So, how do you want to *be* in order to attract who you want to attract? What do you want to give energy to in order to gain more of that?

A Big Fish couple who are very successful business owners keep finding that when they get focused on the business and are on the edge of wild success, they and their friends have lots of tragedy in their lives. After looking at this situation, they found that they got along best when they were dealing with tragedy in their lives. So what was happening is when life was tragic they gave positive energy to each other, when life and business was going well, they would fight and bicker. This pattern set them up for a struggle to success. And what they gave energy to was the struggle – therefore they got more of the same: struggle to success rather than wild success.

A Big Fish whom we will call Paula is the model for giving energy to what you want. Paula, almost 40, is an entrepreneur. Three years ago, she started a massage therapy business. She is a single mom trying to raise her son, and she was not finding enough money to put food on the table. Her business was not doing well. She had just broken up with her boyfriend. Life was bleak. One morning, she called me for a session. She was in tears; her heat and power had been shut off because she was not able to pay the energy bill (notice the irony here!). I think it was the lowest of low days for her, and she was worried about what her son would think when he got home from school; she did not want him to worry.

Paula, after feeling the pain of where she was, *decided* that morning that she was going to pull herself up by her boot straps and change what she was putting her energy toward. This was the day that she became a Big Fish. She chose to switch from giving energy to what was *not* working, to what *was* working. She began actively marketing her business in her neighborhood; she started working out again, regularly; and she committed to a schedule for herself and her son – so that they both had a weekly plan. She took full responsibility for growing her business, stepping into what truly needed to be done to market her business. Now, three years later, she has a thriving practice, she just bought a house and she is married to a wonderful guy. She literally turned her *energy back on* to what would grow her business and not distract from it. Our darkest days are sometimes exactly what we need to help us see the brightest light and possibility. They are our greatest motivators, an inspiration to make drastic change. This is the place where we can find the silver lining in the dark clouds. But we must focus our energy on the silver lining and not let it be pulled into the black hole of the dark clouds. To Paula, the darkest of clouds created the brightest of days. This Big Fish was open enough to take action and take responsibility for her life and her business, rather than to blame and become bitter or angry.

One of the biggest issues that I coach entrepreneurs about is money, or, more specifically, the lack of it. Many books have been written about how we generate wealth and abundance. Entrepreneurs get very caught up in looking at the fact that they don't have enough money; if, instead, they would get excited about how they are going to bring their purpose into the world, they would generate money. Getting paid simply means we are putting our worth out into the world and the world is paying us back. We *decide* how much worth we want to put out into the world.

"To me, money is... almost human. If you treat it with real sympathy and kindness... it will be a good servant... and take care of you." - Katharine Butler Hathaway

Napoleon Hill's book *Think and Grow Rich* reminds us to decide what we want to earn:

"I bargained with life for a penny,
And life would pay no more
However I begged at evening
When I counted my scanty store.

For Life is a just employer,
He gives you what you ask,
But once you have set the wages,
why, you must bear the task.

I worked for a menial's hire,
Only to learn, dismayed,
That any wage I had asked of Life,
Life would have willingly paid."

Earning money is an exchange of energy. This is really an extremely simple concept. When we put our energy into the world where it has value and worth, life pays us back. If the energy we put out into the world is that we do not have enough or life is not fair, or energy of the like, it is that same energy which we get back. A perfect mirror!

The energy we put into the world needs to be shifted from "not enough" to a message of what we offer. From there we create action. Action creates sales. Consistent action creates consistent money flowing in.

Action also creates people saying, "No." And we need that, too, for success. It is not realistic to think that everyone is going to buy, yet generally the reason we do not market ourselves or pick up the phone to initiate a relationship with a potential client is because we do not want to hear that "no." So we tend to do nothing. Nothing creates nothing; a focus on lack of abundance creates more lack of abundance. But a focus on abundance and possibility creates more abundance and possibility. Money and abundance are energy.

It was many years ago, when I was in sales, that I learned every "no" brought me closer to a "yes." Like every salesperson, I knew the odds were that a certain percentage of people to whom I presented my pitch would say, "No," and that another certain percentage would say, "Yes." Then I realized that getting the "no's" out of the way put me closer to reaching those "yeses."

These days, "no's" are perfectly fine with me. I actually appreciate a clear "no" because it lets me move on and look for the next person who wants to be a Big Fish or a Big Fish partner. "No's" also remind me that I am in action and remind me to stay in action!

What I like to have folks do who are feeling a lack is begin to notice, a few times each day, what they are truly grateful for. Make a list; write it down. Also, notice what you *already* have in your life that is abundant. Write that down, too. These may be things you tend to overlook because you take them for granted.

Be grateful for all that you already have. For example, I am grateful every day for my abundance of friends, depth of real conversation with friends, my connection with my family, my brilliant dog and all she teaches me, my health, my abundance of options in how I want to spend my day, the abundance of clients to regularly inspire me, my 'fridge full of food, my choice of cars to drive each day, my lake house, etc. This is the place to begin to create abundance. From here, we continue to manifest more. Of course, it needs to be genuine and honest gratitude.

Keep it simple. If you want more abundance in your life, stop the wanting and start to notice how much abundance you have right now. Then get in action! Turn your energy 180 degrees. It will make all the difference.

In the 21st Century, we are in the mode of buying more and more stuff. Shopping is our number one pastime. But the never-ending desire for more fuels the feeling of "not enough" that is prevalent in our world today. I think we are feeling less fulfilled than ever because of this superficial need to fill up for a temporary feeling of fulfillment. Where did all our abundance go?

I find it ironic that the more we have in America, the less fulfilled we seem to feel as a country. Be a Big Fish. Before you go out shopping, stop and notice all that you already have and enjoy. It may change your spending. The extra stuff is not abundance! We live in a very abundant country and world. Let's appreciate it.

The other place to find abundance is right in front of us, in the little things in life such as the beauty of snow on the trees, crocus coming up in the spring, the smell of lilacs, the taste of a fresh pineapple or a crisp apple, the touch of the fur of a bunny or puppy, the sound of birds chirping in the morning or a moment of silence. This too, is abundance!

"*Inspiration is everywhere. If you're ready to appreciate it, an ant can be one of the wonders of the universe.*" - Author unknown

A Big Fish named Cindy, who had been in the event planning business for years, recently had the realization that there are more important celebrations to create: the celebration of life, death, health and happiness. This came to her from a life-changing trip she took to Africa. On that trip, she kept bumping into the same man; after the third encounter, he asked her if he could take her to his village to show her how they live. She visited the village and has never been the same since. She left her event planning business and is launching a not-for-profit organization dedicated to helping villages in Africa and other third-world countries. She will tell you that ever since she saw how the people in African villages live, she no longer goes to our stores with the same "need to buy," she thinks twice before buying another pair of shoes and she enjoys all that she currently has more than ever. She does not deny that she still loves to shop, but now she savors her purchases so much more – and this switches her energy to a place of abundance, as well.

"Wealth consists not in having great possessions but in having few wants." - Esther de Waal

Stepping back and looking at the big picture of our life can truly help us see our own patterns. I like to think of looking at my life as if from an airplane, up high in the sky. What are the patterns that I am creating? What is the energy that I am putting out into the world? What am I reacting to? What am I taking responsibility for? What am I not taking responsibility for? We have learned to create our own energy patterns: We give energy to certain behavior and not to other behavior, and that creates a cycle in our life and in our relationships both personally and professionally.

I remember where I was when I had the realization that "*everything matters and nothing does.*" I was brushing my teeth one morning in a hotel room where I was staying while attending the last coaching class for my certification. It was at that moment where all of what I had learned seemed to make sense. I was asking myself, "What is this really all about, this thing called life and business… for what reason and why? And how do we make it rich and meaningful each day?" That morning it became crystal clear to me that we need to treat everything in life like it matters and, at the same time, not be attached to any of it. This realization changed my life. It had me live more fully and treat everything and everyone with more respect, care and concern – as well as live lighter at the same time and be able to let it all go. It was a life-changing moment.

What this meant to me is that I could decide what truly matters every day and what really does not. I could decide each moment what I was going to give energy *to* and what I would not give energy to. It was my decision to make.

No one can tell you what "should" matter to you. Only you know that. No one can tell you what does not matter; only you know that, too. But as soon as you are clear that giving your energy to something creates more of the same, you will become much more intentional about what you choose to give your energy to. All of a sudden we step into our own power.

It is, after all, a powerful concept to know that we truly create our own experiences – every single one. We create our successes, we create our failures, we create our reactions to it all. And by what we choose to give energy to, we create more of the same!

Everything does matter. Big Fish treat life with respect. They treat people with respect. They treat themselves with respect. They honor life in all forms. Yet the paradox is that, at the same time, nothing matters. When something does not go like we think it "should," instead of getting irritated and discouraged, we need to trust that there is a greater reason. And consider also that most of the stuff that "matters" has, really, only the importance we choose to give it. It is our interpretation of what is happening, not what is really happening.

A Big Fish named Michael, who owns an advertising firm and is married with three children, has experienced the difference perception can make. He will tell you himself that, at the beginning of our relationship, he used to make mountains out of mole hills. He had financial issues, money was always tight and bills were not getting paid on time. He had high turn-over with his staff. He was working very hard. He was frazzled! Now, he has fully taken charge of creating possibility from each situation rather than being the victim of circumstances. And this Big Fish has manifested a whole new life. He has developed a solid team that backs him up and shares his vision, and he is growing his business exponentially. He no longer simply reacts to life. This Big Fish reminds me weekly that people can change drastically. During the past two years, he has become more and more aware where he is putting his energy. He is a Big Fish!

The following Native American story creates a perfect vision to reinforce this principle:

Cherokee Story
Two Wolves

A Cherokee Elder was teaching his grandchildren about life. He said to them, "A fight is going on inside me... it is a terrible fight between two wolves.

"One wolf represents fear, anger, envy, sorrow, regret, greed, arrogance, self-pity, guilt, resentment, inferiority, lies, false pride and superiority.

"The other stands for joy, peace, love, hope, sharing, serenity, humility, kindness, benevolence, friendship, empathy, generosity, truth, compassion and faith.

"This same fight is going on inside you, and inside every other person, too."

They thought about it for a minute and then one child asked his grandfather,

"Which wolf will win?"

The old man replied simply, "The one you feed."

This principle also works in diminishing behavior that we do not want. This lesson came to me when I got my first dog. The dog trainer advised me that, whenever the dog would do something I did not want her to do, I should not yell at her, not talk to her, not coddle her, but *ignore her*! Dogs want attention, and they learn to do more of whatever gets them that attention. Humans are exactly the same way, so, if we want to change someone's behavior, we must ignore the behavior we do not want and give attention only to the behavior we do want! We need to remember that even angry attention is attention. What the dog trainer did to help me better understand this concept was to have me actually turn my back on my dog when she was doing something I did not want her to do, giving the behavior no attention, then 10 or 20 seconds later give the command again. Giving energy to only what I wanted more of worked in training my dog, and it works just as beautifully for people!

When people are not behaving in ways that are in alignment with where they want to go (the bigger vision), another way to help guide the behavior is to tell them very clearly what you want more of, NOT what they did wrong. Point people toward the behavior that will more quickly move the team toward the vision, rather than beating them up. This shifts the energy from past to future, from wrong to what is possible. It shifts the energy from pushing down to pulling up. It shifts the energy!

Another part of giving energy to that which we want to grow is saying, "No." If we want to raise the bar on the types of clients we are serving, we need to say "no" to all those who are not the ones we want to serve. This allows us to give energy to that which we want more of. And if we want to increase the quality of our work, we need to say "no" to employees who are not producing quality work for our firm. If we want a class act business, we need to say "no" to mediocre.

It is important to understand how the principle of energy affects us in business. We, as entrepreneurs, need to know our strategy and direction. We need to spend our time focusing on growing what is work in our businesses and where we want to go, and not expend all of our energy putting out "fires du jour" or on things that might not even be in sync with our end goals and could ultimately kill our vision by sapping all of our strength and energy.

"*There are two ways of exerting one's strength: one is pushing down, the other is pulling up.*" - Booker T. Washington

Practical Tips and a Writing Exercise:

Identify 3 things that you will ***STOP*** feeding/giving energy to now:

1. ______________________________________

2. ______________________________________

3. ______________________________________

Identify 3 things that you will ***START*** feeding/giving energy to now:

1. ______________________________________

2. ______________________________________

3. ______________________________________

Put the items that you want to feed on your "to do" list for the next 30 days. Take action daily around these items. Begin to truly give them energy, consistently.

"Give energy to that which you want to grow." - Lorin Beller

TWO

Live each day from your vision

This Big Fish principal is about living with the "end in mind," as Wayne Dyer says in his book, *Power of Intention*. We need to be very clear about what we want to create in the world, what we want our impact to be. We get so caught up in email, voice mail and to-do lists that they, rather than our vision, are what run our lives and business, and this is a very tiring place to be. This is where entrepreneurs get burned out, exhausted and finally left wondering, "What is it all about!?"

These days, information comes in, fast and furious; we cannot even try to keep up with it in real time. I receive 75+ email messages per day, and at least a half-dozen voice mail messages, and I schedule at least ten appointments via phone. If I get caught up only in keeping up with the minutiae, I lose sight – or even consciousness – of my vision.

There is a critical paradox that Big Fish know, and that is, "*In order to really go fast, we need to slow down!*" We need to think and listen to ourselves more before acting. We need to do much more thinking and listening to our hearts so that, when we do act, those actions will be bigger and bolder. We will talk more about this in chapter seven when we discuss bold actions.

So, while it seems a contradiction, in order to get off this hamster wheel of how we are working each day, we need to step back and look way out into the future. Look out ten or twenty years. What do you see? What impact do you want to have in the world with your business? What impact do you want to have on your family? What impact do you want to have on the environment?

Many people do not think about this; we are generally very myopic people. But step back and look at the bigger picture of your life. Be proactive about where you are going, not reactive. After all, WE GET TO CHOOSE WHERE WE ARE GOING. Yes, it is true. We get to choose our vision!

Beautifully illustrating this concept is a story from *Write It Down, Make It Happen* by Henriette Anne Klauser. "Jim Carrey walked up to the Hollywood Hills and wrote a check to himself for ten million dollars. On the memo line, he wrote, 'For Services Rendered.' For years, the comedian carried the check around with him, long before he was ever paid that kind of money for a movie. Now he is one of the highest-paid entertainers in the industry, getting twenty million dollars for a film."

If you are not able to see your vision, look higher. And if you are still not able to see it, look even higher. Your vision is like the sun – it is ALWAYS there, you just have to get above the clouds. Every single time I have ever been in an airplane during daylight hours, we get above the clouds and POP! there is the sun. You just might be choosing to stay stuck in the clouds. Of course, that is also a choice, and it is okay if you are okay with it. If not, go higher and find the sun – your vision – every single day!

"A man, to carry on a successful business, must have imagination. He must see things as in a vision, a dream of the whole thing." - Charles Schwab

A Big Fish married couple own a jewelry store. They are work partners and life partners, and they have two young-adult children. His strengths are vision and large picture work. Her strengths are sales and implementation of the short-term plans and programs. He was generally scattered and all over the board. She was constantly frustrated with his lack of initiative. Then he wrote his vision story (10 years out), and found he needed to change how he was working *today* because how he was working was not *aligned* with where he wanted to go. The process shifted everything in the present. What he realized was that his vision is not about selling jewelry; the store is the vehicle to his real passion, which is having an impact in the community. Now you will hear, on radio and TV, commercials that talk about the community and the impact he wants to have in the world. The couple is doing creative marketing that is sending a message to the community that their business is interested in what is happening in their local community. They are working from the end, and that vision has impact on today.

I have always loved the story about the convict who was in prison for twenty years. He loved golf. For twenty years, he played golf in his mind. He visualized being out on the golf course again, and he practiced in his mind, playing 18 holes a day for twenty years. The weather was always perfect, the sun was always shining, and the course was always impeccable. After twenty years in prison, he walked out of prison and played the best game of golf he had ever played in real life. Our mind, our vision, of what we can do is limitless. Having a vision has huge impact.

Wayne Dyer says, "*Believe it and you'll see it; know it and you'll be it.*"

This premise is critical. I am not talking about dreaming about your future. I am talking about *knowing*. Know that you can create your vision. It takes just as much energy to create a lousy vision as it does to create a great one! So what is your vision for your company? What is your vision for your life? Notice your energy: Do you get excited about your vision? Or is your vision so daunting that it does not inspire you? Big Fish choose visions that inspire them. Having a vision inspires and raises our energy every single day. We keep the vision in our mind's eye, and then we give energy to it. Imagine that! Giving energy to our vision creates it!

It is also important that your vision is written or visual, not simply a thought. Remember, in the first chapter, the written word (and pictures, too) have energy. So writing about or creating an image of your vision increases the energy you are giving your vision.

Once you have documented your vision, it is important to keep it with you. In other words, post it at your desk or in a place where you will see it often.

When I was in my early twenties, the minister of the church I attended told a story about a picture of Mt. Hood she had in her office years ago. She loved that photo. After looking at the photo in her office for some years, she was offered a new ministry job that she took – and upon getting settled in her new office, she found that her view outside her window was Mt. Hood! Talk about creating what we want! She envisioned her view and it was created! This is why we need to be careful what we ask for; we just might get it!

Having our vision where we can look at it helps us keep our eyes on the higher vision instead of the day-to-day to-do list. In fact, continuing to look at the to-do list often creates frazzled entrepreneurs and frazzled employees. I did this when I owned my technology company. I was driving myself and my team insane by my wild to-do lists. Since then, I have learned that giving energy to our vision tends to inspire and increase our energy naturally. It is obvious which one keeps the momentum going.

Magic happens when we create a vision for our business and life and then back it up with action and a plan. We can see proof of this in the following research: In 1953, Yale University conducted a study of its graduates. For twenty years the subjects were interviewed and tracked. The results showed that the top 3 percent earned more money than the other 97 percent *combined.* And the only difference between the individuals was that the first group had written goals AND a plan of action to achieve them. Harvard did a similar study of its business school graduates in 1979. They found that 84 percent of the class had no goals at all other than "to have fun and enjoy themselves" – in other words, to live life by chance. Thirteen percent had goals but had not created a plan, while the remaining 3 percent had written goals and a plan of action. The results showed that the 13 percent earned more than the 84 percent without goals, and that the 3 percent earned more than ten times the 97 percent *combined.*

Big Fish have *written* plans!

What I have seen in Big Fish and also experienced personally is that once we know where we are going in life and business, the process is easier. We are more focused. We are more determined. And we allow less to distract us. We are clearer about what we say "no" to and clearer about what we say "yes" to. When this shift happens, we are suddenly more aligned with where we want to go in life.

Recently, I had the opportunity to hear Mrs. Fields speak about her business. She said her father had always told her, "*True wealth is family, friends and loving what you do.*" I bring this up because so many people get caught up in the money alone. And just having or striving for the money is a very lonely place to be. From our vision, we can create money, but I have not yet met one Big Fish whose vision contained only a goal of reaching a certain number in the checkbook. There is so much that is of the same or greater value to us. When we hold on too tightly to the need to make money, we lose sight of all else that is important.

Years ago, in my early 20s, I created a collage of my vision. It was a fun project. My collage was filled with cut-outs of pictures of things I wanted do, possessions I wanted to have, the number of clients I wanted, the number of employees that worked at the technology firm that I owned with my former husband, etc. When I look back now at that collage, it amazes me because I have done just about all that I had wanted to do, have acquired most of what I cut out pictures of, have traveled to many of the places on the travel list and have taken my business just about where I had envisioned.

The funniest part of this story is that when my former husband and I wrote a business plan for the bank for the same business, they turned us down for the loan. The business plan was not even as aggressive as the numbers in my journal, yet those were the numbers that were most accurate. Why? I believe it is because they were written not just from basic math but from my intuition as well. The bank was looking strictly at numbers and did not understand the industry.

It is a powerful and freeing experience to have a written vision for your business and life. Have fun with creating the vision. Be sure it inspires you.

The collage vision is also the tool that kept me moving forward when times were challenging. I *knew* in my heart that if I just kept going it would manifest as I saw it in my mind's eye, or even better. At the same time, I knew that if it did not, there was a bigger and better reason for it – and I was open to learning from my current vision.

The basic premise is that we need to know what our intentions are. We need to be conscious of what we want to create in the world, and then be open to allowing the world to create it with us. Setting intention that a vision is going to manifest is stepping into it with a knowing. I like to think about creating an intention of "this or something better" so that we leave the world open to creating at *least* what we are envisioning – sometimes a whole lot better! So many entrepreneurs I know create a vision and then either let it go completely and do not set the intention, or do the opposite, holding onto it so tightly that there is no room to creatively create it. So, create your vision and set the intention that your vision will manifest. We must believe it! And if it does not come to be, we need to look at what is in the way of the believing.

This principle is about living as though that which you want to create is *already* here! Think about energy: If we are living as though the vision is already here, we begin to attract it.

But you cannot live this way for the sake of the vision. You have to live this way for the sake of loving today, loving what you have already created in your life, your business, your world. And if you are not loving your life and business, then it is critical that you change it now. Immediately, your energy will change. And when your energy is transformed, you will be living from a place of higher energy – and this begins to feel like your vision! It comes full circle.

What typically gets in the way of believing is fear of some sort: fear of success, fear of failure, fear of embarrassment, fear of what others will think, fear of not being good enough, etc. It is important to acknowledge what is in the way of believing in our vision. Journal on it; write until you can see a new perspective about the vision. Most of the time we try to ignore the fear, but when we ignore it, it rules us. *What we cannot be with rules us!* So I encourage writing about your fears until you find out that there is nothing to fear. Write, write, write until you find possibility beyond the fear. But when you do this, your intention is critical – you are writing to release fear. If writing does not work, get a coach and coach around it – have the coach help find new perspectives around the situation. This will be a freeing exercise, guaranteed!

The paradox about having a vision is that it is not about the vision – it is about this moment! It is about today and how we choose to live today! Today turns into tomorrow. Therefore, it is critical that we live today in a way that will enable us to create tomorrow's vision.

The question that will help you know if you are living and working from this principle is: "Is what I am doing today, this moment, moving me *toward* my vision or away from my vision?" If you are able to answer consistently, "toward," then your actions are aligned with your vision. Not being able to answer the question that way is a great awareness, and shows you it is time to re-align.

If you are driving a car that is out of alignment, it is more work to keep it on the road. It pulls to one side or the other, it shakes and wobbles. But if your car is in perfect alignment, it is easier on your hands and arms to keep it on the path that you intend to follow.

This principle is used every day when sailing a boat. When we sail a boat, we constantly get off course. What enables us reach our destination is the consistent action of getting back on course. In every moment, we must stay alert to whether or not our actions will take us where we want to go. By checking our course, we can determine that and adjust our sails (our actions) accordingly.

Consistency in our actions has huge impact. Consistent flowing water is the *only thing* that created the Grand Canyon. Great things are created with consistent action. When our actions are not consistent, they are diluted – inconsistent – and such behavior has limited impact and limited results.

We do not know what we are capable of until we are asked. I believe this is why we need to have a coach or someone in that role who consistently challenges us. When we are challenged in a loving, supportive way, we find out what we are capable of – and that assists us in creating our vision.

Bob Nardelli, CEO of Home Depot, has said, "*I absolutely believe that people, unless coached, never reach their maximum capabilities.*"

The interesting concept in the above statement is that our strength of purpose is beyond who we are. In other words, when we know our purpose in life, it is bigger than we are; and when we are clear about that purpose and can see the vision clearly, that, in and of itself, motivates us to continue to go forward. The coach or support person constantly raises the bar and assists us in gaining clarity.

Another important point about vision is that in Corporate America, or, for that matter, any organization, it is the CEO's and/or leader's responsibility for setting the vision, and collaborating with the team to have them participate and contribute to that vision. If, as a leader, we do not take responsibility for the vision, people get tired and they lose interest, and we find the organization gets stagnant. Vision is a natural motivator – people love to know where they are going. They also love to participate in the direction. Setting a clear vision will also weed out those who are not on board with the vision, and that, too, is a critical step. You don't want to keep someone on the team if they are not inspired by the vision, because they will distract from the energy of moving forward.

"Where there is no vision, the people perish." – Proverbs

In business language, to summarize, it is critical to have a plan, commit it to both paper and people, and make sure it evolves dynamically as you work against it each day. Start TODAY – not tomorrow, not next week, not next quarter.

Practical Tips and a Writing Exercise:

Take some time and write about your vision. These questions will help you get started, but feel free to add your own.

Where do you want to be in 10, 20, 30 years?
What do you want to have experienced?
What is the difference you want to have made?
What do you want to have?
What do you want to see?
Where do you want to go?
What is the tone of your life?
What is the speed at which you move?
What is the view out of your office?
What is the temperature of the places you live?
What are you eating for lunch?
What is the smell outside?
What sounds do hear each morning?

____
____
____
____
____
____
____.

Now that your vision is written, refer to it often! Convert the written word to the visual collage if you are a visual person. Post it some place where you will see it regularly. Look at it often, allow it to have the inspiration, power and focus that it can have on you.

"If you do follow your bliss,
you put yourself on a kind of track
that has been there all the while waiting for you,
and the life you ought to be living
is the one you are living.
When you can see that,
you begin to meet people
who are in the field of your bliss,
and they open the doors to you.
I say, follow your bliss and don't be afraid,
and doors will open
where you didn't know they were going to be.
If you follow your bliss,
doors will open for you that wouldn't have opened for anyone else."

- Joseph Campbell

THREE

To truly change your world,
you cannot let the world change you.

This principle is directly related to the first principle: Give energy to that which you want to grow. What this new principle means is that we need to know so well who we are at our core that we do not let anything or anyone shake us. When we allow others to shake us in any way, we are in that moment not being who we truly are.

I believe that at our core, we, Big Fish, want to do good things for others, we want to make a difference in other people's lives and in the world, we want to get along with each other, we want peace in our lives and in the world, we want to feel good, we want to have fun and we want to experience the fullness of life. What sometimes happens is someone or something enters our world or our lives that causes us to feel badly. We REACT to that person or incident rather than stay true to ourselves. That reaction is negative energy coming from our false self, or ego, which has just been hurt in some way. The Big Fish challenge is to not let the world change you when the world is being topsy-turvy all around you.

So, who are you at your core? Most of us at our core are full of love, happiness, fun, trust and possibility. It is when the rug is pulled out from under us that we tend to let all that go and immediately become full of resentment, anger, jealously and hatred. Our Big Fish mission, then, is to remain true to our core even when people are not thoughtful, even when people do and say mean things, even when tragedy happens, even when we are scared and hurt, even when we are facing the unknown and even when things to go one way when we expected them to go another. This is truly something to practice and be conscious of.

Let me be very clear – I am not talking about being a floor mat and letting people walk on you. *ABSOLUTELY NOT.* Big Fish do not get walked on! Big Fish set clear limits and boundaries for themselves, but from a place of love and not of fear. In other words, we often become rigid and set rules and boundaries because we are angry or because someone did not do their job and we are trying to punish them. Those rules and boundaries tend to make our life small, literally and figuratively, and reduce possibility – because they come from a source that is low energy. Rather than setting rules and boundaries from anger, set them from a place of love and possibility and what we want more of from that person. These two scenarios create very different results.

One Big Fish I just started working with decided to enroll in the program because his business was hard and he continued to have run-ins with his clients and colleagues. Shortly into the coaching relationship, it was evident that he was letting his clients and colleagues rock his boat. If they did something he did not agree with, he would get upset and frustrated and feel walked upon. Bottom line: He let them walk on him. What they did is not the issue;

no one can walk on us unless we let them! He is now beginning to see that he is giving energy to their lousy behavior, and that is getting him more of the same – behavior that gets him easily frustrated.
The first step, here, is to notice that our behavior cannot match the behavior of the frustrating client; instead, the behavior needs to immediately trigger a switch of the energy from frustrated and angry to possibility. This Big Fish reminds me regularly how tangled we get in our roles, rather than standing firmly in who we want to be in this world. In order to become who we want to be, we need to have a clear vision of what we want to create.

People tend to challenge this principle because they do not see how they can escape being affected by those who are 'causing them conflict.' So, let's look at conflict simply. Generally, what happens is that, when we get in a discussion with someone, we immediately feel the pull and tug going on. So we first need to stop and notice that we just got into a pull and tug situation. To me, this pull and tug is like putting a fence between us and we are shouting between the fence posts. If we are able to notice, we can consciously get on the same side of the fence with that person. I recently heard someone say that in order to change someone's mind, we first have to understand their mind. So, from this frustrated place, it is a great indicator that it is time to get very curious and understand where they are standing – not agree or disagree but just understand, meet them where they are and from there, together, both parties can create the next place to go. If the fence remains between you, nothing will ever change. This behavior is powerful and will enable you to create relationships that are a win-win.

These tug and pull relationships happen among corporate teams, with our clients, with our vendors and with our life partners! And the tug and pull is an indicator that we just put that fence between us and it is time for us to get back on the same side of the fence, get curious and learn much more about where their mind is rather than trying to insist the other person see where our mind is. Again, this is about energy.

Let's look at another metaphor to further clarify this point. If we can visualize two perspectives of two different people as different colored beach balls, this situation is like trying to push the beach balls into each others arms and face when we are each holding our own beach ball. What Big Fish do is temporarily put down our own beach ball and learn about the other person's beach ball first. Then, when they are ready – which actually happens rather quickly when we do this – we introduce them to our beach ball and begin to work together on creating a vision as to how both beach balls can be used in the game or how we might use just one because we both agree on one after exploring both beach balls. The simplicity here is being done for a reason. Our opinions are just that, like beach balls. It is our *attachment* to them that gives them more meaning to us. It is our ego that has us need to have our beach ball be seen by others. When we are focused on the greater vision, what we are trying to accomplish – as long as we stay firm in our values

– it does not matter how we get there. Big Fish want to empower others to get to our end result – that is what really matters.

"When you talk, you repeat what you already know; when you listen, you often learn something." - Jared Sparks, historian and editor

A Big Fish, Julie, owns a not-for-profit organization she and her father started that is dedicated to helping at-risk youth launch companies and supporting them in entrepreneurship. A year ago, she would have told you that she did not have time to work out, that taking care of herself was not the priority. She has three daughters and is married; work and family came first, Julie last. She has a large vision for impacting our world. The other day her computer totally fried – what I think is one of the most frustrating experiences we have in business these days – yet she remained calm, cool and collected. She noticed this reaction, recognizing that a year ago, she would have been a basket case for the entire time the computer was not working, and been frustrated with people, arguing with them and pushing them to move faster to fix it.

This time, Julie chose to go with the flow, get the system fixed and move on. She wasted much less energy, and worked toward a solution rather than making herself crazy over a situation that actually was calling for her to stand firm and work with people to fix the problem. After a year in the Big Fish program, Julie is calmer and is even taking better care of herself by working out in the gym 3 to 5 times a week for an hour. When her computer fried, she worked out rather than ranting and raving. She is happier, and she is running her business more intentionally from a place of positive thoughts and what is possible. She is also running it like a company rather than a shoe-string organization. This Big Fish has transformed herself and her business!

Underlying this principle is the idea that we need to know ourselves. We need to know who we are, and when we do, we stand firmly in our full authenticity and power – just the opposite of being walked on and taken advantage of.

Thomas Jefferson said, "*Swim with the current - stand like a rock.*" This is exactly what this principle is about.

In order to stand firm, the paradox here is that we need to better understand others! Usually, rather than standing firm, we will argue and defend our perspective, and that gets us 'thrown off course.' If, instead, we stopped, became more curious and tried to better understand the other's perspective during conflict, we would actually have our boats rocked less! Our egos tend to say, "No way," and want to fight for our positive or perspective – and that actually makes us lose the ground that we really want to be standing on. When we take the time to learn and meet people where they are, from there we have much more influence in creating a firm place to stand.

The person in the room who understands all perspectives honestly is the most powerful person in the room! This takes letting go of what we think is right or wrong and letting go of the concept that there is only one way to accomplish a task. Here is a fun picture that helps illustrate this point.

Lady or Lizard?

I was at dinner recently with two friends. We were talking about the *Today* show. I knew that my one friend has been a fan of the *Today* show for years, and I had happened to see it that day asked her if she had seen it also. She quickly responded, "No. I won't watch that show any more!" I was surprised at her response. She proceeded to tell me that she had sent in an application for a contest, and she had spent a lot of time on it. After many months had passed, they chose someone else for the contest. My friend thought they really *should* have taken the time to write a thank you note to all who had sent in long, involved applications. Because the *Today* show did not acknowledge the applicants, she was angry at them and would no longer watch the show.

I do not have an opinion as to whether she is right or wrong. What I want to point out is, who really is the inconvenienced person? My friend liked the show, or so she said. Did she let the world change her? Did she let her judgments and ego make this decision? Or did she make it from the core of who she wants to be? (Only she can answer these questions.)

One rule of thumb I use is, does the decision make my world smaller or bigger? Does the decision exclude people and things from my life or does it include more that help create more possibility? In my friend's case, does the *Today* show know or even care that she is no longer watching? Who truly knows? And what is she giving energy to in this scenario? One could say that she is giving energy to not being acknowledged, or we could say that she is no longer giving energy to the *Today* show.

Another response that might have let my friend remain true to herself more fully would have been to write a short letter to the *Today* show explaining to them that she was disappointed to have spent so much time on her application and not to have even gotten a letter of rejection that thanked her for submitting it. When we help people know what we want more of from them, we are much more apt to get what we want and need. And communicating this helps us stay true to ourselves more consistently

Big Fish don't have internal judges.

How do we know if we are acting from judgment or out of ego, anger, frustration or the like? Listen to ourselves: Do we find ourselves using phrases such as "they *should* have" or "they *could* have"? This is a quick indicator that we are judging and blaming, rather than accepting others for who they are and standing like a rock in who we are. It also puts us in a place of looking at our past, which is behind us, and that will not ever serve our vision. In order to stand firm in who we are, we need to communicate more, not less. Switch the energy to the vision by looking at what you want *more of from* the person and, just as important, from *yourself*! Point them and you in that direction and you begin to serve your vision and have your actions of today impact your vision of tomorrow. This also results in your taking responsibility for your vision and your behavior today rather than blaming yesterday's behavior and spending time on that. That would be wasted energy, in both time and money!

David Roth, a singer and songwriter, wrote an entertaining song, *Don't should on me*. It is a fun song that mocks a relationship between a couple who have been together a while, and how they have "shoulds" for how each "should" behave toward the other. Thanks to this song, every time I hear someone use the word "should," it makes me more aware of what we are doing to ourselves and/or to others when we use it.

A Big Fish, Robin, has owned a company for the last 11 years. She reported that she is happier now than she has ever been before because she recently learned to clearly say and ask for what she wants. She went on to explain that she does this from a place of *joy*, not from a place of looking for approval or out of obligation. If we are doing things for approval or obligation, we are not doing them from a place of joy. For the first time in her life, she is excited about her own life, and this is having a positive impact on her relationship with employees, customers, husband and son. She is paying attention and she is taking action, and together those two things have her walking around wanting to express her excitement. Naturally, from this place she is inspiring others to be happy. It is the domino effect.

Anger, frustration and emotions like them are the best emotions to tell us that someone is either stepping on something of value to us or the world is challenging us to see a new perspective. Recently, I have become clearer about using these times to either be more communicative about what I want next time and/or to see the bigger picture of what I am really frustrated with and learn from it. These emotions serve us when we can use them to create clarity.

These emotions, however, absolutely do not serve us if we stay in them for any length of time and relive the situation over and over again. Our bodies do not know the difference between the actual event in real life and the relived event in our mind, and these negative emotions create real stress in our bodies. This is exactly the type of behavior that leads to headaches, stomach aches, heart attacks, strokes and other health challenges! It is not the situation that is bad for us; what is bad is us choosing to relive it over and over and over. This is old news; we know that stress is not healthy for us.

The Big Fish place to work and live from is where we choose quickly and stand like a rock *authentically*! The key word here is "authentically." If we stand firm but are still angry, that does not count! We need to stand firm in our hearts and in our actions. We need to give energy to the perspective that serves our vision, not the perspective that has us angry and frustrated. This takes practice, it takes constant knowing who we are, and it takes consistent effort to keep our vision in our mind's eye. This is a mental place that many Big Fish visit often. It is the place where we untangle the two wolves of the parable presented in the first chapter of this book.

Another Big Fish, Mary Ann, who is a medical doctor, chose to give up a thriving practice to share what she felt was information that would have greater impact in the world than what she could contribute working with people one on one. Now, she is a public speaker and author, sharing information that has great impact for every parent in our world. She is working really hard to get her message out to the world. She is not selling a lot of books *yet*, nor has she yet gotten that big speaking engagement that will make her wildly successful. It has been an uphill battle. She is not getting full support from family and friends, yet she is not letting the world get in the way of her vision and her mission. She continues to move forward a little bit every single day.

She and I both know that with such consistent behavior, she is well on her way to being wildly successful. It is her initiative that is so important these days in our fast-paced world. Some people would run into a road block and stop. Feel defeated. Give up. She did not, nor is she letting the world change her behavior. I know that her determination, her actions and her dedication to herself and her mission will take her to wild places. She is a Big Fish and she continues to not let the world change her. And when the world does get in her way, she reaches out to her Big Fish community who remind her of her vision and encourage her to keep on her path.

Recently, I had the opportunity to hear Maya Angelou speak. She said, *"Change the things you do not like. If you cannot, change the way you think about them."* We cannot make life and business work the way we want them to. We cannot make the world work the way we want it to. And actually, that is a great gift because it would be way too much work if we could! So if we decide that we do not like something and, rather than living with it resentfully, change the way we think about it – we create a very happy life!

Maya Angelou ended her talk with the statement and the title of her book, "*I shall not be moved.*" What simple, powerful advice. Know what you stand for, know what you want in your heart, know why you are standing firm in this place and *do not be moved*!

We tend to not take the time to know ourselves very well and, therefore, we can be moved all over the place. Rather than driving our own boats, we tend to become like the toys that get pulled behind boats. We let others drive us! We get pulled all over the water. What this principle calls us to do is to know ourselves so well that we drive our own boats in our life. We direct *us* in each moment. This takes being more awake to who we are first and foremost, then choosing our response from that *knowing place* rather than the other way around.

Many new Big Fish tend to do very well when they are making a lot of money, but the instant the money is not flowing or abundant, they go to a grumpy, frustrated, panicked place. When we do this, we interrupt the flow of money coming into us. We let the world influence our mood and our attitude. It is important to understand that the lack of consistency in our attitude and action has a huge impact on our clients, our staff, our customers, our families, etc. We think that people do not notice. They do! And that attitude impacts new monies, new opportunities and new possibilities coming into our companies. If we truly want to change our world and become more abundant in all aspects of ourselves, we need to not let the world change us! To consistently not be moved creates constant money flow and an abundance of clients, work and jobs coming in!

Let us also look at how we let others make us happy, too – the flip side of what we have been talking about. A friend of mine told me that when a certain person came into his life for a day or a few days, he was happy, and when that person left, he was no longer happy. You see, *we* make it all about people or a special person. Those people, personal friends or work colleagues, represent something to us. *IT IS NOT ABOUT THE INDIVIDUAL PEOPLE.*

In business, new clients give us hope and a feeling of success. In our personal lives, people with whom we enjoy hanging around support our values such as family, fun, adventure, connection with others and with ourselves, etc. We make it all about the other people, and when they are no longer filling that place, we tend to say the relationship is no longer working for us. But we cannot let others create our happiness, or our unhappiness for that matter. We get to create that for ourselves.

Another example of this comes from the person who inspired me to write this book. He did so by being grumpy day after day. I watched him unhappy, angry, sad and gloomy. The way he was choosing to live his life inspired me to share my knowledge with people, to help them know that they are totally in charge of their lives and businesses. Do I want to see him happy? Yes, more than anything. And he represents to me all those in the world who choose to suffer or be miserable regularly. It is not about him and it is all about him *and* what he represented to me to inspire me to be the writer I had never before seen myself being.

Recently, I had a business meeting with a potential Big Fish marketing partner. That potential partner wanted me to change my brand, change my pricing, change the class content, change the books that we read, etc. I listened. I was curious about what they *really* wanted. What they wanted was: money, the appearance that they owned the brand, and fitting the Big Fish way into their way. To me, it was like putting a square peg in a round hole. I had to stand like a rock, honor and respect what they were bringing to the table, and say, "Thank you but no thank you." When we are clear with our visions we more easily say no to things, relationships and opportunities that take us off track. No's are sometimes more critical than yeses. No's keep our path streamlined. No's lead to more time in our lives and more space for opportunities that are more fitting for us and our vision.

To conclude, this principle is about staying grounded in who you are so that you can go exactly where you want to go in your life without letting others influence that. One of my good friends used a line the other day that I love. She said, "I have found the wings on my feet." And that to me says it all when it comes to this principle. We need to stay grounded in who we are, our values, our passions, our purpose and our vision, and from there we can fly and not let others knock us off course. With wings on our feet we can go anywhere, we can do anything. We become in integrity with ourselves and take wild leaps all at the same time. This is truly living fully.

First, we need to be clear as to how we want to change the world (at least our world) and what the impact is that we want to have as a leader (entrepreneur). When we get clear about our impact, then we are better at deciding what choices to make in our response to people that we allow to push our buttons.

In business terms, it is critical to stay solid in your vision and actions. This doesn't mean ignoring sage business advice, but don't let it rule you! Heed your gut, your heart and your head.

Practical Tips and a Writing Exercise:

What is the impact you want to have in the world?

____
____
____
____
____
____
____
____
____
____.

What will be your new Big Fish way of responding next time your buttons get pushed?

____
____
____
____

____.

What do you need to do regularly that grounds you?

____.

Whatever it is that you wrote down in the last question – things that ground you – put that on your to-do list every day for the next 30 days. Integrate that which grounds you into your daily life. Take action consistently on it.

"*Go within every day and find the inner strength so that the world will not blow your candle out.*" - Katherine Dunham

FOUR

Dance between responsibility of creating your vision and having faith that it will unfold naturally. In the meantime, live fully.

First, as we discussed in chapter two, it is an important premise that Big Fish have a vision for their lives (personally and professionally). When we have a vision that we are passionate about, it drives us. It is our North Star. It is our anchor that keeps us grounded. We also are responsible for carrying out that vision, manifesting it, creating it. We do not expect anyone else to do it for us. This fourth principal is about how we hold our vision in our mind's eye. We are fully responsible for the vision and at the same time we have faith that it will unfold.

David Roth, a wonderfully talented folk singer and songwriter, has a song called *Rising in Love*. One of the lines in the song says, *"A bird in the hand will stay until you start to close your fingers around it."* This is how we need to hold our vision: gently and *open*, as if holding a live bird in the hand. Not tightly, for when we are so attached to *how* it should look, we strangle the creative universal process and, for that matter, our own process!

When I worked at my Internet company, my nickname was "Make It Happen Beller." When someone had a challenge, they would bring it to me and, together, we would come up with a plan to "make it happen." Life was a lot of work. I was like a bull in a china store or a bulldozer – making things happen and sometimes not even realizing what I was climbing over to create it! I was so attached to "making it happen" I was missing life. I was missing the magic in the world. I was so focused on making things happen a certain way that I was working much harder than I needed to.

Dr. Seuss, in his book *Oh the Places You'll Go,* points out that when we set an intention, it will take us to wild, magical and scary places. And that journey is what it is all about. The intention matters, but the journey matters more. The intention is what gets us on the journey in the first place.

The paradox is that we must keep our eye on the vision and, at the same time, let it go enough to allow it to unfold in the world with us. This takes *trust* and *patience*. These are two skills or two characteristics that we humans in the Twenty-First Century have not mastered. Big Fish continue to refine these skills. What we find is that the more we trust, the more we can trust. The more we practice patience, the more quickly things manifest in our lives! It takes honestly stepping up to the plate and using and practicing these skills, like we would if we were practicing soccer drills or learning to play an instrument. Practice. Consciously practice.

Let us take a closer look at trust. There are many kinds of trust. We can trust that our staff or our partner (personal or professional) is competent in doing the skills that we need them to do or want them to do. This is an important trust. This kind of trust is often the kind we look for when interviewing potential employees. We look for the skill that they can do the job. We look for experience in a certain skill. We look for training in a certain skill. We also look for certain skills in life partners, too. A friend recently told me he wanted a partner who cooked. The skill of cooking was high on the list of traits he wanted in his next partner. We look for ability to do a job, then trust that the person will actually do it. This is a basic trust we either have of each other or not.

We want to trust that people can do the job, whatever it is, and when we cannot it changes the dynamics of a relationship. At work, for instance, if someone begins to not do certain skills/jobs that we expected them to, we find out that we cannot trust that person to do any part of the job we *assumed* that they would. This is a basic trust, and it's important in running an office – we need to know that we can trust that certain things will be accomplished. This is one kind of trust, and it is limiting.

However, there is a deeper trust. That is a trust of knowing that we are able to rely on others and also to *be reliable to* others. That is the kind of trust that, when the road is rocky, lets us know the other person will be there standing by our side supporting us and getting through the challenge with us. We may think this trust is one we should reserve for spouses or significant others, but we also need to have this in our business partners, our vendors, our clients and our support staff. This kind of trust has employees showing up when things in the office are especially challenging. This is the kind of trust that keeps us moving forward. But if we want others to fulfill this trust for us, we need to fulfill this trust for them, too. This kind of trust is about *commitment* to a relationship in the hard times and the easy times for the sake of the relationship and the sake of the *vision* that the relationship will create.

Through this kind of trust, also, we know that the other person's actions match their words. This is the kind of trust that makes one a Big Fish! This is the kind of trust that Big Fish are building with others. This is knowing that others can count on our word and we can count on theirs. This kind of trust builds businesses that have the solidest foundation. This is about being in integrity with ourselves and, at the same time, being in integrity with each other. We all know people who, when they say they will do something, always follow through. Their word is one that can be counted on no matter what. I would bet, too, that these people are successful and happy in their own way, whatever that is, because these people keep their word to themselves, too. These are Big Fish!

Many leaders and entrepreneurs believe that we build teams from a place of fear. Organizations built on fear-based trust fall apart quickly. Fear has people looking over their shoulder; it has them begin to look elsewhere for jobs; and it has people feeling like they are walking on eggshells. This is just one way of leading; in my mind, it's the "old way." The new approach, which we can switch to as a leader any time we want, is to lead from a place of support and trust. When we are leading from this place, whether it is in our own one person company or a Fortune 100 firm or our family unit, we can change it!! It takes responsibility to your word. *Every word.* You can start this change today! It is that simple.

Big Fish mean what they say and say what they mean!

Dr. Seuss was one of our great teachers via his children's books, and one book that I love is *Horton Hatches the Egg*. Horton, the elephant, agrees to sit on an egg while the mother goes gallivanting all over the world without a care or a sense of responsibility to her egg. Horton's continued commitment to sit on that egg through thick and thin had a huge impact. He would say, "I'll stay on this egg. I meant what I said and said what I meant… And elephant's faith is one hundred percent!" The story ends with something brand new – an elephant bird. Because of Horton's commitment and his being faithful to his word, they sent him home *happy* one hundred percent with his new elephant bird!

The moral of this story is that when we can count on ourselves and our word, we are "*happy, one hundred percent.*" This is full responsibility!

This is how committed to our word we need to be as Big Fish. People learn that they can trust us. And vice versa. This behavior creates faith – faith in ourselves first and foremost, and faith in each other. When we lose faith in each other, there is all the more reason to go back and have greater faith in ourselves.

This behavior has us also know that we can count on ourselves. And there is no one more important for us to know we can count on!

Let's be clear: This does not mean we cannot change our mind. We can. But we need to communicate it! We need to let the other party know if we made a mistake, and take responsibility for that, too!

Most of the time, if we can trust a person's word and their actions match their words, we have basic integrity and trust between us. When that happens, other forms of trust fall into place. On the other hand, you can have a trust only in someone's skills without the other ways of trusting. This is the case for most of Corporate America! What would happen to our large companies if we could help them build integrity trust from the top down? I dare say we would have a happier Corporate America.

Big Fish know that their words matter in all relationships, personally and professionally. You see, when others can count on our words, we, too, can count on our words. And when we know we can count on ourselves, we feel better about who we are – and we know that what we say we are going to do, we will do. The more we do what we say, the better we feel about who we are. It is a wonderful cycle that has us rise up rather than spiral down.

Someone once said that since we have the Statue of Liberty on the East Coast, we should have the Statue of Responsibility on the West Coast. In the United States, we can create a life in any way we want. This is true freedom. But we cannot have freedom without responsibility. The freedom to create a vision comes with responsibility to that vision. I see them as statues on each side of our vision, like book ends.

Another thing important to Big Fish is *confidence*. Because confidence is not something we can buy in a store or a bottle, let us look at where it does come from and how we grow it or give energy to it.
Confidence comes from exploring, trying new things, venturing out and finding out that when we do these things we survive! We trust ourselves to take care of ourselves in a situation and trust that others are there if we need them. When we can trust ourselves that we are doing the best we can, we become more confident in ourselves. Confidence comes from finding that of which we are afraid, and diving in! Confidence comes from learning about our world, all aspects of it. Confidence is expanded when we expand our learning about ourselves and the world around us. The more we explore our world, the bigger our world gets and the more confident we become in it. Confidence comes from always knowing where our home base is, our grounded place.

"*Real confidence comes from knowing and accepting yourself--your strengths and your limitations--in contrast to depending on affirmation from others.*" - Judith M. Bardwick, sociologist

"Having faith" is also part of this principle. Trusting that all will happen as it is supposed to. There was one event in my life that helped me see how important it is to have faith. I was 16 years old and for that summer I stayed for six weeks with family friends in Montauk, Long Island. The dad of the family was a fisherman, out at 3 or 4 in the morning to get the fish as the sun came up. I wanted to catch a lobster. Stacy, the Dad, got me a lobster pot and told me that it was my responsibility to check that pot daily. Each morning I would go out early and check that pot with full faith that one day there would be lobsters in that pot. Each day, it was the same: light and easy to pull up. The summer weather was getting cooler and soon it would be time to go home and back to school.

One morning, I checked the lobster pot and I could not lift it. I called Stacy for help, and he came running. I'll never forget it; he said, "Kid you got some lobsters!" I was so excited! As I looked more closely, I saw there were six of them in that pot and they had the rubber bands on them just like in the grocery store. I wondered how those lobsters got in. I asked Stacy what he thought, and he proceeded to tell me that he heard from other fisherman that morning that a shoot broke at a local restaurant and many lobsters got dumped back in the water. I was one of the lucky ones to get six of them. (Did I say that there were six mouths to feed that night?!) Stacy let me believe that I had legitimately caught those lobsters. I learned in that moment that if I could imagine it, it could happen. It does not matter if it is "set up" or not; it matters that when we believe, it can happen.

This summer, 22 years later, I was having dinner with the same wonderful family and I asked Stacy to look me in the eye and tell me how those lobsters got in my pot. He looked me square in the eye and said, "I put those lobsters in that pot." With tears in my eyes from that pure gesture of love, I realized at that moment that he had taught me that having faith matters – that it does not matter how, it matters what we are having faith in. The bottom line of this true story is we can walk around with faith in our hearts and trust that what we believe *is* possible or we can walk around in our worlds and not believe and not have faith and trust. We get to choose! Thank goodness for me, I was taught early on that if I believed, I could achieve! I have built wildly successful businesses on that concept!

The last part of this principle is critical – it is the part that says "live fully!" In other words, when we have a vision, we must keep our eye on it and we must also trust that the world will co-create it with us. But we don't waste time while we are waiting; we use that time to the fullest. So many people say, "I will take that trip when…" Or "I will spend time with my family when…" Or "I will take Fridays off when…" We put off fully living until we reach some age or monetary goal, or a significant person comes into our life. The Big Fish challenge is to live fully NOW. There is no time like the present. This is truly the only time we have – this moment. This does not mean over-spending or not doing our work. It does mean integrating being responsible for our vision with living fully, too.

This is the principle that allows for *wild fun*! When we develop a compelling vision that calls us forth each day, we tend to clarify our to-do list and streamline our work. We are clearer about what we say "yes" to and what we say "no" to. When this happens, we have more time on our hands for other important things such as taking care of ourselves, traveling, spending time with family, etc. The bottom line is that we have more time for fun, more time for play! This is where we begin to fully live!

"Live each present moment completely and the future will take care of itself, fully enjoy the wonder and beauty of each instant." - Yogi Paramahansa Yogananda

I made a decision to travel more this year. I decided that rather than do marketing from the comfort of my desk, I would attend large conferences, both national and international. It has actually made my business more successful! And I am spending the same marketing budget! You see, when we begin to look at what is possible way out there 10 years away, we can close the gap and re-arrange our life today like we want it to work. We get stuck in a place thinking that it must be this way until... until now! Until we realize that we can create our lives more like we want it right now! It takes getting out of our own way, out of our box – looking at what we REALLY want, being innovative and creative, and walking our own path.

Who says we need to work 8-6, five days per week? Whose rule is that? Why are we choosing to follow society's unspoken rules or the rules of the norm? Running in that pack tends to have us blend in and do life the "gray" way. Be a Big Fish; do it *your* way – a colorful way that suits you AND serves your customers, clients and family, too!

"Change the way we look at things and the things we look at change," Wayne Dyer says.

What also happens here is that there is less of a distinction between work and play. We get to play at work and work during play, and life begins to have fewer lines and boxes around how we function. Our lives are more integrated. When we live like this we tend to have more impact, too. We meet great contacts for work while playing, and work tends to have a lot more fun in it. This also helps us retain employees. When we are fun, we tend to attract more people. They want to be around us, and they are motivated, too.

If we are able to truly trust we are also able to fully live. Naturally, trusting allows us to live. This is total freedom. From this place, the world is our oyster and anything is possible. It is from this place that our vision begins to come alive. It is also from this place that we live without fear.

I can help underscore a very practical way of thinking about this principle by telling a story of a Big Fish. She is a jewelry designer in California. After she created her vision as a Big Fish, the next step was to have her create the written plan to back up that vision. When she did, she chose to be in *action* immediately. It created wild results; she was on fire. She started being proactive in getting her name out into the world, and others helped her – including her fellow Big Fish – and she got national corporate orders for her work. She totally stepped into this principle. She took responsibility for her vision (took action) and maintained her faith that it would manifest. She also fully enjoyed the process in the meantime, living fully. She created incredible results for herself during her first year in business.

Big Fish begin to see themselves and their potential in the world, and they fill that space. Like real fish! Did you know that koi, when put in a small tank, will grow only so big, but when that same fish is put in a large tank, it will grow proportionately to the size of the tank? Put that same fish in a pond and it will grow even bigger! So you decide: How big do you want your tank? You get to decide how big your tank is because the tank is as big as you want it to be.

I like to think of this analogy as living fully. In other words, what would have you live fully? What would need to be present in your life (material things or not!) to feel as though you are living fully? Hold that vision, be responsible for it and have faith that it will manifest. In the meantime, live as though it already was present in your life; live fully. And voilà – you will be surprised how big you grow.

A Big Fish named Sue owns a successful veterinary practice in upstate New York. She and I were talking about what would make her life bigger and she thought that I meant increasing her business size or doubling her client base. That is not what I meant at all. What I was asking was, "What would have you feel like you are living your big life?" What she realized was that living her "big life" was actually getting her practice in New York running really well, streamlining it, having it be very efficient and opening another practice in another state so that she could spend summers in New York and winters in a warmer part of the country, alternating where she lived every six months for the next ten years. That was her "big life" and her big vision for herself. Big does not necessarily mean bigger. It means as great as it can be for you. Your own big life – your life with the volume turned all the way up on fully living – that is big! Bigger is not always better; better might be smaller, simpler. Big Fish get to decide what their Big Fish life truly is; no one else gets to define it but you!

Finally, this principle also has us know that the only thing we really have is time. We get to choose in each moment how we spend it. As I write this paragraph, it is what would have been my grandmother's 90th birthday. The morning of the day that she had a stroke – the beginning of the end of her life – I received a message in my email that said, "What would you do if you had one hour left?" Those words remind me regularly how precious life is and that we truly get to *choose* in each moment how we spend our time. I *choose*, now, to live even more fully every single day.

Do we want to spend our time loving life fully or do we want to spend it complaining about yesterday? Do we want to use it to accomplish our vision or move farther away from our vision? Do we want to build people up with our time or push them down? Do we want to be comfortable or do we want to stretch? We get to choose, and that, too, is an abundant place to stand. In other words, in each moment we are truly free; we have so many choices! This is true abundance. All we have is time. And we never know how much of that we have. We tend to live like we have a lot of it rather than living like we have a limited supply.

Or said another way, "*We act like life was certain and death uncertain. Life is uncertain and death is certain.*"
- The Reverend Jesse Jackson, spoken in a eulogy for Ennis Cosby

The business importance here is that it is critical to have plans and strategy but also to stay tuned-in to the natural and ever-changing rhythm of business and cultural environments. Know that some of this ebb and flow will help grow your business and some will pose challenges. Also, in the meantime don't work yourself literally to the bone. Enjoy life, see a friend, spend time with family, work out and play. Live fully.

"*Time is too slow for those who wait, too swift for those who fear, too long for those who grieve, too short for those who rejoice, but for those who love, time is eternity.*"
- Henry Van Dyke

Practical Tips and a Writing Exercise:

What 10 things is it time to take responsibility for if I am going to create my vision?

1. ______________________________

2. ______________________________

3. ______________________________

4. ______________________________

5. ____

6. ____

7. ____

8. ____

9. ____

10. ____

What is it time to have more trust in?

____
____
____
____
____
____
____
____
____
____
____.

Is my word as good as it gets? _______ If not, what will it take for me to be 100% responsible for my word?

____
____
____
____
____

What will I do to live more fully today?

What will I do to live more fully this week? (Put this in your to-do list to remind you.)

What will I do to live more fully this month? (Put this on your to-do list to remind you.)

____.

What will I do to live more fully this year? (Put this on your to-do list to remind you.)

____.

What will I do to live more fully every day? (Put this on your to-do list to remind you to do for the next 30 days.)

"*The price of greatness is responsibility.*" - Winston Churchill

FIVE

Always be kind before being right.

One of the biggest challenges that I hear about when working with entrepreneurs is the challenge of working with others. It's a common issue, and I remember when I was in the corporate world that a workshop which always attracted a large attendance was "How to deal with difficult people." Think about the energy of that statement! Guess what we are going to get more of: difficult people! This challenge exists in our homes, our communities, our work place – big or small – and in our world.

Our competitive culture tends to be fear-based rather than empowering-based. The principle we discuss in this chapter creates a much more cooperative culture rather than a competitive one. We can change entire cultures by using this formula.

Often the only reason we cannot be kind is that we are too attached to our own perspective. And if we are "right," the other party must be "wrong." I believe the most powerful person in the room is the one who sees all perspectives and, from that place of conflict, can establish creativity and then productivity. The *conflict* is attacked quickly and efficiently, not the people; we continue to be kind to the people! In this place we keep our energy on the present and the vision (goal), not on the history. The focus is win-win!

Big Fish tend to be kind people; at the very least they *want* to be. They have come to the realization that life is about living from a place of understanding, compassion and love. If we are truly committed to living a more peaceful life, there is no room for "right or wrong."

After all, if there is no wrong, there is also no right. And if there is neither right nor wrong, then we can begin to get more curious about various perspectives, even those with which we might not agree, and use that curiosity for the purpose of exploring, expanding and learning. From this place we tend to design what works for both parties from a perspective of creating a win-win situation rather than blaming each other.

Think about the energy of the two words "kind" and "right." They have very different energy. In my mind, "right" has a struggle to it – one person is right and one is wrong. If we give attention to this energy, guess what we get more of: struggle! But "kind," in my mind, has a more empowering energy to it. If we switch our energy to "kind," we empower other people – and we move more quickly toward our vision and theirs! It's simple: You get to choose what you want to give energy to.

Another way to say this is that in order to create winners, we do *not* have to have a loser. I prefer to see how we can truly create kindness and winners all around. If we can hold the challenge like a puzzle to be solved rather than a fight to be won, it changes the energy of the entire situation. Sprinkle a bit of kindness in the next struggle and see what might be created.

If the goal is to win at all costs, we leave a bloody mess. If the goal is to enjoy the process of the game and win fairly, we both end up winners because we enjoyed the game – and our time. It can be a challenging principle for some people. This is the point at which Big Fish interact with others in the world. Through this principle, Big Fish create highly productive partnerships, both personally and professionally. This principle also has us remove our egos and dig deeper to find compassion. It is because of our egos wanting to be right that we make others wrong or we find fault. Everything we do as humans, we do to make ourselves feel better, feel happy.

This is an important point: *Everything we do, we do to make ourselves feel happy.*

That includes making others wrong, going to war, slapping a child, killing someone and, on the other hand, helping someone, giving a gift, etc. We do things because we want to feel good or because we do not want to feel guilty, or because we think we should or that it's the right thing to do.

However, what truly makes us happy is living from the vision of compassion, love and having a positive impact on others. This is a universal desire in Big Fish – to have a positive impact on the world. When we rise above the fault-finding and critical, judgmental thinking of others and look for how we can be kind and compassionate, we tend to have a more peaceful life and more success. This relates back to principle number one, in that if we give energy to the right-or-wrong situation instead of being kind and compassionate, guess what we get more of!? You've got it: *Whatever you give attention and energy to grows!*

So many times I think that we are hung up on being right, *dead right*. Yet, what do we get from hanging onto being right? What benefits come from it?

Until we stop and ask ourselves those questions, we'll continue to treat proving that we are right as a life or death issue. But we have the power to change that. It's like when I am playing tug of war with a dog – we can only play until one of us drops the rope. As soon as that happens, the game is over. As long as we want to continue to be right, we are hanging onto the rope. Big Fish drop the rope first. They choose to be kind before being right.

Recently, I was privileged to hear Maya Angelou speak. She said, "*Never whine, it lets the brute know that a victim is in the neighborhood.*" She went on to say, "*Your adversaries can't take it when you laugh.*" Finally, she said, "*When you are in the catbird seat – be kind!*"

I do not believe that Maya Angelou intended us to not communicate or to laugh. I believe she intended us to communicate, but for reasons that come from our desire to be kinder. However, this does not mean to not acknowledge our anger. Anger can be a great messenger that one of our deep values is getting stepped on. For example, I tend to get angry when I am not treated with basic respect. I use such situations to help people know when they are not treating me – and usually others as well – with respect. I see anger as a red flag for a learning moment and sometimes a teaching moment. And I take it as a time to share about myself for the sake of creating more Big Fish in the world and for the sake of me creating more quality relationships in my life.

Another point that is critical here, again, is that *everything matters, and nothing does.* From this place, it is much easier to see things that you can laugh at! What I mean by this is, everything does matter, which is why our kind words and actions are so important. And when things are not as planned, Big Fish know that there is a bigger plan. Keep on being kind and open, and find an attitude of "What is about to unfold here?" What's past does not matter; roll with it. Be fluid. Be flexible. Find an attitude of wonder in it all. Big Fish know that *everything matters and nothing does*.

Focusing on being right takes us off track of our vision. It has us not take care of ourselves. It has us give our own power away. On the surface, it has us momentarily think that we are standing more firmly in our power, but if we are not walking our own path to our own vision, we are not walking in our true power. Let us look at the challenge of taking care of ourselves. It is a critical component to being a Big Fish. If we do not take care of ourselves on our journey to our vision, we might not have the energy and stamina to get there.

There is a lot of talk these days about work-life balance, and this conversation actually creates more of an issue. Let me explain what I mean. First of all, our society places a high value on working – the more we work, the more the boss might pay us or the bigger our bonus might be or we might get that promotion or our spouse will stop nagging us about chores around the house. The complaining itself actually wastes time and energy! When I was working in Corporate America a number of years ago, we talked so much about how much work we had to do, it seemed that we never really got much accomplished!

Another thing we tend to do is segregate our life into isolated realms: work, home, family, recreation, health. I believe that is a disservice. This compartmentalized way of thinking has us more stressed. It has us trying to fit things into separate little boxes. Big Fish flow from one aspect of their lives to another when it is natural, not just because the clock says so or social mores dictate something.

Big Fish create balance by living fully, doing what they want to do when they feel like doing it, but with discipline. For example, you might find Big Fish working out at the gym in the middle of the work day because that is when they are at their peak or it clears their mind for the afternoon. You also may find Big Fish being a bit more spontaneous when something strikes them in the moment that seems like it will serve the greater vision.

This is an important concept: The vision is held and, while living fully, we begin to be more aware of what is happening around us. If we are too focused on the mission, we will become oblivious to our surroundings, to people, beauty and opportunities, too.

Big Fish have a structure and discipline, but hold it loosely in case something shows up that even better serves their vision.

"*Discipline is the guardrail that keeps you on the path of self-esteem.*" - Kent Nelson

Part of self-awareness is taking care of ourselves. The more we become aware of our responsibility and ability to live fully in this life, the more we know how critical it is to take care of ourselves in all ways. Then the act of working out will no longer be a challenge. Having our values stepped on will not be tolerated. There are many ways we take care of ourselves – when we are more aware of who we are, we *want* to take care our minds, bodies and our energy.

These days, I am living fully and I am taking very good care of myself. I exercise regularly by skiing or kayaking during the week. I have a cook who creates healthy meals for me. I travel for my work and see the world. I enjoy friends often and I love my work. I choose to get bodywork (massage and chiropractic work) regularly to take care of my body, and I choose to read and take relaxing time regularly.

I have had numerous people say to me, "I am living vicariously through you," and my response is often, "DON'T!" Your life is about being alive and living fully. If you find yourself living fully through someone else, that is a GREAT tip that there is room to turn up the volume on living your OWN life more fully. What would your business be like if you turned up the volume on living fully toward your vision??

I was having dinner with a friend recently who is a financial advisor for a large firm, and he was telling me that if he does not *love* his clients, *he fires them*. He proceeded to explain that it is more important to him to love his clients than to recruit clients with lots of money. He added that he had a client who had only a very small amount of money that she invested with him. But he enjoyed working with her. She referred another client to him who referred another – and eventually, through all her referrals, that very small bank account turned into $1.3 million in business via referrals. What a great example of how important it is to be kind, and love our work and our clients.

When it is easy to be kind, kindness follows. Working only with clients that we love is a bold move, but one that I believe pays off over and over again. The other part of this is that we can look for reasons to love our clients rather than judge them!

What we are talking about in this principle is real conversation – from our hearts, not from our egos or wallets. We want to initiate inviting conversation instead of antagonistic conversation. This is an art, not a science. I cannot write the steps down as to how to do this; it comes from practice. It comes from listening truly to the other person and at the same time to our hearts and what our hearts are curious about and what our hearts want to say. It is being *vulnerable* and *honest*, which is not something for which there is much room in Corporate America today. It is putting ourselves on the line and being authentic.

A Big Fish was talking about how she was finding that being more open to sharing what she needs for herself was leaving her feeling a bit vulnerable, and that was not comfortable. But at the same time, she was finding that being vulnerable with others had them sharing more about who they were, and from there they were designing relationships that were more of a natural win-win. Amazing!

Usually, as leaders we tend to not be vulnerable. We think it is a sign of weakness or lack of leadership, so the Big Fish challenge is to become more vulnerable and more open about ourselves and our vision. Explore it. Try it. Check it out. Be curious about where it could lead.

Vulnerability and honesty create real conversation, which creates room to try something new. This creates room for learning, room to exceed limits more than we ever would have, and it creates room to fail and learn from that failure.

"*Our greatest glory is not in never failing, but in rising up every time we fail.*" - Ralph Waldo Emerson

The beautiful thing about this principle is that you get to choose what you want to give energy to! In other words, do we want to give energy to being right or to being kind? It's all about energy.

The past couple of decades there has been a lot of talk about changing the office culture. But simply put, the office culture that exists in a company is tied to what the leader of the company gives energy to. The entrepreneur/leader of the company or department absolutely sets the tone for the culture. What that person gives energy to trickles into the entire company – every nook and cranny, every pore. So if you are that leader, it is critical that you be clear on what you want as your office culture and to pay attention to directing your energy to that culture – and not to something else. If there is something in your office culture that you do not like, look into your own actions or thoughts to see how you are consciously or unconsciously giving energy to it. Begin to notice.

When I was working in a corporate job as Vice President of Sales and Marketing for a technology firm that acquired my company, I was on the integration team. We acquired 13 companies over the course of 2.5 years. What I loved about each company was their individual culture and how the owners of each firm absolutely created that culture whether they knew it or not. The challenge was honoring the current culture while also merging it to the corporate culture. I have to say, we did not do this well. I believe that the opportunity and key to successful mergers is to honor the old culture – be kind to it, not judge it and not try to change it quickly. Allow it to have impact on the new and the new to have impact on it. Have a clear intention on what the two entities are moving toward. When we are merging two entities, whether it is two companies or adding new staff, we need to first become clear on what the strengths are of each of the parties, what influence we want them to have on each other – rather than simply trying to put a square peg into a round whole, which only creates mergers that tend to not have long term success. When we are clear on each party's value, we can honor it; we can allow it to have influence on the other entity and vice versa. From this place we create a much stronger single entity that serves better over all. There is a sense of each party being honored and feeling valued rather than one being "right" and the other "wrong."

This principle is also tied to Principle Number Two: Work from the end in mind. If we can imagine ourselves at the end of our life looking back at how we treated people, I believe that we will want to have treated others with kindness and compassion rather than with judgment and critical behavior. So if we are living today from the end in mind, wouldn't we like to look back and know that we were kind?

What would your relationships look like if you were setting out each day to find kindness rather than another person right or wrong? How do we motivate and inspire from the place of kindness? I believe it starts with curiosity. When we shift our energy from judgment to curiosity, we can begin to understand – and it is only from this place of meeting people where they are that we can shift and inspire.

My mother taught me when I was a child that if we really wanted to know how someone else feels, we need to take off our own shoes and put their shoes on. The way that I do this is to ask questions from a place of curiosity. Such questions begin with *what* rather than *why*. With this curious approach we tend to create more meaningful relationships. From the place of "What did you see in that situation?" we get to see where they are. And they feel you have really seen them. From there, we can design what we both want more of. This is giving energy to the win-win in the relationship rather than the struggle in the relationship.

If I feel I am right, and determine in my mind that someone else is wrong, then I am judging them. When I sense it, I try to counter that tendency by asking a "what" question such as: "What has you see it that way?" "What do you want more of?" "What is working for you in the situation?" "What is not working for you?"

Part of being curious is listening to the other person. If we are truly listening, we can demonstrate it by *doing* something based on what we hear. People then feel heard and acknowledged. This is true kindness – being the mirror for the greatness that we see in others.

Being kind before being right is, I believe, the seedling for peace in our world. If we all began to live this principle we would have less war and fighting, and more peace and honoring of each other.

The other part of this is the energy that you give the conversation. Is it heavy and serious or is the energy light and open? A more playful tone gets far better results than that serious, more judgmental tone.

A friend recently told me how he empowered one of his key employees in his corporation. Even though his words were serious (and a bit judgmental), he was able to create a relaxed and empowering situation because his tone was totally fun and playful.

Our tones can be kind and playful. We can play with relationships, swing out and have fun, and at the same time (back to chapter number four), be responsible. If you make a mess because of your playful way of interacting, stick around to clean it up – after all, that is what Big Fish do!

Another friend of mine says, "Do I want to be happy or right?" You choose! I love this thought. We get to decide: Does our ego need to prove ourselves right or do we choose to let go of that struggle and be happy?! It is truly simple. Right? Or happy?

There is another perspective to this principle: Those who have been kind to us ought to be saluted regularly! They are our cheerleaders, our supporters, our allies; and they are our courage and confidence when we may lose ours temporarily. Big Fish honor and salute those who have been kind to us over the course of the days, weeks, months, years and lifetime. Those relationships are worth more than any amount of money in the world. These are the people who help us continue to strive for our vision and our possibilities. Take them with you in your heart wherever you go. You can call upon them when you need them.

When I was 17 years old and left for college, a basketball coach of mine sent me $20 the first month of school with a note that said, "Have a few drinks on me. Love, D.T." That note meant so much to me at that stage in my life, when I was not really supported by adult male figures, encouraging me to go off and explore the world. That small act of kindness and support has led to years and years of a relationship that has been one of the most supportive relationships in my life. His friendship and kindness have been there throughout my life in subtle yet powerful ways. More than twenty years later, we continue to maintain a relationship that inspires both of us to raise the bar for each other. He continues to be a cheerleader and support for me, and sent me a note just last week that said, "Get that book done, so I can read it, and help sell it... for the greater good." You never know what a small act of kindness will have on another person's life and how it comes back always, full circle.

Business-wise, the bottom line with this principle is that how we treat customers, employees and vendors is critical. Those who put people (their wishes, goals, hot buttons, etc.) first over power trips or dollar signs usually come out on top in the long run.

Practical Tips and a Writing Exercise:

Next time you find yourself saying, "That is not right" or "That is wrong," what do you want your response to be?

____

____

____

____

____.

What 3 questions might you ask in a situation where you recognize that what you are doing is finding right and wrong? Post these questions someplace that serves you.

(I have the following statement on my bathroom mirror, "Good Morning, this is God. I will be handling all your problems today. I do not need your help. So relax and enjoy the day.")

1. ____

2. ____

3. ____

"*The highest form of wisdom is kindness.*" - The Talmud

SIX

Trust that perfection is all around you right now.

This principle reminds me each day of the magic in our world. The more we live these principles, the more magic we see. There is perfection in everything, we just need to look for it and notice it.

This is where we need to be much more *innovative* in our approach to work and life. This is where we need to get out of our own way and do things differently than we have ever done before. If something in your business or life is frustrating or feels like it is a pattern, it is a wonderful red flag screaming to get your attention so you will notice what is NOT working. It's your signal to look for a very new approach to accomplishing what you are trying to accomplish. This is where we need coaches to help us find the new way. Alone, we continue to step into our own patterns and habits. On our own, we tend to not find a new way. Professional coaches help us find a new path to reaching our goal that is much more efficient, through a process that helps us break old patterns.

The following story illustrates behavior that we all fall prey to, all too often: If you put fleas in a large jar with the top off, over time they will all jump out of that jar. If you put the same fleas in a jar and put the top on for an extended period of time and then remove the top, they will not jump out of the jar. You see, we put our own tops on our jars!

We create our own glass ceilings! We think that we cannot change until someone gives us room to. And that simply is not true, if we want to become wildly successful. Notice what you want more of – from this current place you are in. Be grateful that you just stopped and noticed! Then ask yourself: What do you I want more of? Most of the time, what we want more of is seen in our visions. From this place of what we want more of, get clear, VERY CLEAR about what it is we want more of and go create it. Create it from a place of possibility not a place of making it hard.

Creating our visions is easy when we keep our attention on it, the vision, and not get distracted by the obstacles. I like to think of the obstacles as events or experiences that we need to "lean into" rather than try to avoid… if we are flowing down a river on a raft, if we relax, we will naturally go around the obstacle. It is when we try and fight the obstacle that it becomes more work. I was and still can be now and again, a master at making it hard. And when I realized how simple and easy creating and manifesting truly is – I remember giggling for days, weeks – and I am still giggling! Trust that the obstacle has purpose, and there is perfection in its time in showing up in your life and business – be sure to learn from it. And lean in, let go, be unattached to it. Enjoy the journey.

A movie that came out recently, *What the Bleep Do We Know*, is about the potential of human consciousness and how we are fully responsible for our lives. My favorite line of the movie is at the end, when one character asks another if he will be going to the party that evening and the other character says, "Yes. Shall I bring my chains?" (he was referring to the chains that hold us down and limit our potential) and the first character says, "Of course; we always do!" We are the limiting people in our own lives, not others. Until we take responsibility for our own chains, our lives will be smaller, more frustrating and limiting. Big Fish decide that it is time to move about the world without chains, without holding onto anything and with a true sense of freedom. The perfection in this is from finally seeing our own chains! From that moment, life will never be the same again.

I remember that moment in my life. I was 16 years old and had just read Scott Peck's book, *The Road Less Traveled.* This book is about discipline, love, growth and grace. When I closed the book, I was so inspired by it I wrote a letter (handwritten, because computers were not here yet) and thanked Scott Peck for his book. I had become committed to creating my own life, not the life that someone else wanted for me. He wrote back, thanking me and encouraging me to continue on that path. It was a defining moment. And I continue to have more and more clarity around walking my own path in many areas of my life. It happens in an instant. And we continue to gain more and more clarity as we stay on that path and notice where we do have perfection and where we do not have perfection. But the real perfection is that we notice!

There is perfection in a flower opening up each morning. In the summer, I have hundreds of day lilies that close each night at sundown and open each morning at sunrise; that is perfection! And how does this apply to creating perfection in our lives? IT IS ALL PERFECTION! How can the flowers open each morning and the rest not be perfect too?

Have you ever noticed that you received the money or the account at the perfect time to cover an expense that you did not expect? Or the perfect employee walked through the door to apply for the job opening that you just spoke to someone about? Or the timing of getting a contract or client came at the perfect time of meeting a particular vendor? That is perfection. Notice it, be grateful for it, and honor it.

It is hard sometimes to see the perfection when we are struggling. Many Big Fish with whom I work, myself included, tend to make the process harder than it needs to be. We focus on what is not working rather than on what is working. And guess what!? We get more of what is not working!

Find what *is* working. Find the perfection in your day, every day. Even if it was "one of those days." I guarantee you that in every single day there is perfection somewhere waiting to be spotted.

If something happens in the morning and you say, "It is going to be one of those days…," stop! As soon as you notice that you are saying that, begin to look for the perfection in what just happened. Switch the energy immediately.

My great friend and colleague Samy Chong says, "*At any given moment, you are one thought away from being happy.*" As long as we are *aware* of the bigger mission that we are seeking, and we stay in the *present* moment, we can *decide* to change the thought, which will change the behavior, too.

You see, behaviors do not just happen. They are directly related to our thoughts, beliefs and what we *know*. So if our thoughts, beliefs and what we think we *know* are limiting, guess what? We create limiting behaviors that give us results that we do not like or results that are not satisfying to us. This will happen over and over and over again. This is generally the place I find most entrepreneurs are in when they are ready to be Big Fish. They are doing the same thing over and over and expecting different results. This is the perfect formula for frustration!

What we need to do is change the thought or the belief or the knowing. From there, behavior changes, and when we change behavior we create different results.

It is all about energy, to go back to principle number one. The thought, belief or knowing is just a form of energy. We choose whether to make it limiting or empowering. When we act or behave from a limiting energy, we receive limiting results. The same concept is true when we act or behave from an empowering energy – we receive empowering results. We need to be very aware of the energy of our thoughts, beliefs and knowing.

Let's look at the difference between a thought, a belief and a knowing. (All, by the way, lead to similar behaviors.) Webster defines a thought as, "a developed intention or plan." Webster also defines a belief as, "a state or habit of mind in which trust or confidence is placed in some person or thing." And a knowing is, "personal knowledge." All of these, by the way, are energy. And remember, from the first chapter, what we give energy to grows. If our thoughts, beliefs and knowing is energy… the more aware we are of our beliefs, knowing and thoughts the more we can create our future.

What we need to do is find our true knowing. Generally we *know* deep in our hearts. We do not know why, we just know. Our thoughts and beliefs come from our heads. Therefore, thoughts and beliefs can change, whereas knowing, generally, does not. We stand more firmly in knowings. We also tend to not trust ourselves here, so it is here that Big Fish must learn to trust ourselves more! This distinction is subtle and critical. Wayne Dyer's words help underscore this point: "*Believe it and you'll see it; know it and you'll be it.*"

So if you think that you will see perfection, you will. If you think you will not, you are right in that, too! You get to choose!

I like to think of it as a "seek and find" game. And the more challenging the day, the more fun to find perfection! It is a perspective shift. But Big Fish know how to do that well!

It is the tragedy that we see in the world, I think, that has folks buck this principle. Let's take just one tragedy: September 11, 2001. This was a tremendous tragedy. The lives that were lost, thc lives that will never be the same, the lives that had so much potential, the children who are less one parent or two, the parents who lost children, the loves that lost loves, the loss of freedom that we are currently living with – it is all incredibly sad. I want to acknowledge the sadness and honor those who go on and live more challenging lives because of that tragedy. Their lives will never be the same because of that day. My heart goes out to them still today. At the same time, I have to say more people living today are choosing to *fully live* because of this tragedy. It became, for many, a wake up call to live more fully?

There is a wonderful quote by Brian Andreas, an American artist and storyteller: "*Most people don't know there are angels whose only job is to make sure you don't get too comfortable and fall asleep and miss your life.*" It may help us to consider the people whose livcs were lost or whose lives will never be the same as our angels to wake us up and help us make sure to not miss our life. I like to think of folks who have come into my life, inspired change and walked away, as angels as well.

I am privileged to work with a Big Fish named Kelly, who was a Wall Street executive at the time of the 9/11 tragedy. That incident made her take a close look at her life. She decided that her work was not fulfilling. She was not truly happy on Wall Street. So she left, and opened a retail shop on a waterfront town in New Jersey, selling hand-made artistic pieces for the home. She is very successful just a few years later. She was awakened by the tragedy to live more fully. *That is perfection.*

There are hundreds and thousands of stories such as this one from the tragic events of September 11, 2001. More people are choosing lives and businesses that make them happier, and in which they can have more impact. When we have more happy people in our world, we begin to also have more peace in our world. That is pure perfection.

I have begun to see pain this way: Pain is the messenger telling us it is time for change. Pain is the messenger that is trying to tell us to learn something and change. If it is painful to get out of bed in the morning – literally or figuratively – it is time for change! If we dislike work so much that it is painful, it is time for change! If we continue to experience pain, it is our *responsibility* to search for a new way – a new vision! If we do not change our behavior, pain can be a form of punishment. Why would we keep doing the same thing over and over and over if we are still in pain? I believe pain is a messenger to tell us to let go of the past, the old way of doing it (whatever 'it' is). *Pain* is the *messenger* telling you that it is time to set yourself *free* right now!

Tragedy is pain, and it happens every day somewhere. We get to choose to see the darkness of that tragedy or find the lightness of it. The perfection is in seeing both the darkness and the lightness. The darkness is the inspiration to see the lightness. There is a time and place for seeing both. In other words, I believe that we need to know the deep sadness of such events to finally get to the place of seeing the possibility and the lightness that incident created.

When we are in pain, we need to allow the pain in. This allows more space for love in the future. It is when we hold onto the pain – cover it up, not allow ourselves to experience, carry it with us – that we do not allow for healing and love to come from it.

Business can be painful. We experience struggle and loss. When we stop to notice that we are in a struggle, that is when we begin to see perfection. In other words, when we stop to notice that the business we are running or the life we are running is painful, and we take responsibility for that and begin to look for perfection, then we can move from that painful, challenging, hard place to a place of ease, possibility and fun! This is the point where we begin to see perfection in all places in our lives.

The following story, by an anonymous writer, is a great example of the fact that we have an abundance of choice of perspective.

One day a father of a very wealthy family took his son on a trip to the country with the express purpose of showing his son how poor people live. They spent a couple of days and nights on the farm of what would be considered a very poor family.

On their return from their trip, the father asked his son, "How was the trip?"

"It was great, Dad."

"Did you see how poor people live?" the father asked.

"Oh, yeah," said the son.

"So, tell me, what did you learn from the trip?" asked the father.

The son answered: "I saw that we have one dog and they had four. We have a pool that reaches to the middle of our garden and they have a creek that has no end. We have imported lanterns in our garden and they have the stars at night. Our patio reaches to the front yard and they have the whole horizon. We have a small piece of land to live on and they have fields that go beyond our sight. We have servants who serve us, but they serve others. We buy our food, but they grow theirs. We have walls around our property to protect us, they have friends to protect them."

The boy's father was speechless.

Then his son added, "Thanks, Dad, for showing me how poor we are."

Isn't perspective a wonderful thing? Makes you wonder what would happen if we all gave thanks for everything we have, instead of worrying about what we don't have.

You see there is no such thing as one perspective being right and another being wrong; both are what they are. If we are able to see various perspectives, we are richer for having so many choices. It is when we are stuck at one choice that we feel limited and small.

I was working, recently, with a Big Fish named Paul. He is in the financial planning industry in California. Paul set high goals for himself this year. Up to March, it had been a challenging year. All of a sudden, things shifted drastically. From an intern he had helped with no thought of getting anything back for himself, he received a very large lead and referral. Then, someone in his firm chose to leave and this Big Fish was the recipient of his book of business. These two things changed his business dramatically. But he looked at his situation from a place of fear, saying he was "afraid to count on any of it" because it might then go away, rather than the perspective of being absolutely grateful for what had been dropped in his lap! We switched the energy from that of holding back to that of being utterly grateful.

Remember, give energy to that which we want more of and trust that perfection is all around right now. Even when it appears not so perfect, it is! Big Fish are grateful and show it and speak their gratitude.

"*Feeling gratitude and not expressing it is like wrapping a present and not giving it.*" - William Arthur Ward

Another important concept has to do with the concept of good and great. Jim Collins' book, *From Good to Great*, deals with this topic. His point is that we tend to see things as "good" or as mediocre and this has us play small, not see our possibilities and lower our bar. "Great," on the other hand, as Jim Collins points out, is what separates regular fish from Big Fish, great companies from mediocre ones. The enemy of great is good! I challenge you to go beyond good. If we settle for "good enough" and choose to see just the good, we do not strive to create great! *Our visions are great! Do not settle for good!* Find perfection! Big Fish look for creating great! They raise the bar and go for the gold – and create great!

"Don't be afraid to give up the good to go for the great."
- John D. Rockefeller

Another time to look for perfection is when we cannot make a decision. I was in Florida not long ago and was trying to decide whether or not to go on a trip with a friend. It would be a great adventure, but there were also some good reasons to not go. My thinking had me standing exactly in the middle between saying, "Yes, go" and, "No, don't go." I decided to throw the decision out to the world. In the morning, while out running, I saw a boat in the water with the name "Y KNOT." I smiled, said, "Thank you," and made up my mind that I would go on the trip. In order to see perfection, we need to be aware of the world around us and unattached to the outcome.

Perfection exists every single day in beautiful ways. When I see perfection, I smile at the beauty of it and am in awe each time. In order to see perfection, we need to acknowledge our feelings of frustration, guilt and anger then let them go. Those feelings tend to blind us from seeing the perfection, and letting them go is what creates the space in our life to see it.

Applied to business, this principle says that when you're on the treadmill of business you can sometimes lose sight of what's working or what has potential, and spend 24 hours per day 7 days per week pulled into what's broken. Be present for what is working in your business and your life, and see that some of the "all important" broken stuff might not even feed your ultimate goal or be worthy of all your attention and energy.

Practical Tips and a Writing Exercise:

Be a Big Fish. Jot down a challenging situation that might have you stuck. Play with it; find 5 different perspectives from which you can look at it.

First, describe the situation.

____
____
____
____
____
____
____
____.

Find 5 different perspectives on it.

1. ____

2. ____

3. ____

4. ____

5. ____

Choose one perspective from the above list to live in today that is different from the one in which you have been standing.

____
____
____
____
____
____.

Where is the perfection in your world? Find it.

____
____
____
____
____
____
____
____
____
____
____
____.

Now lighten up! Go with the flow. Take it easy. Relax. Limber up and have fun. Smile. Today is the only day you have.

"*As soon as you trust yourself, you will know how to live.*"
- Johann Wolfgang von Goethe

SEVEN

*Choose your attitude and your actions, and **boldly act**!*

Part of being an entrepreneur is taking action. We tend to act the same way all the time, and this creates the same results. If you want different results, act differently. Most of the time, we act mildly. What would happen if we acted boldly? I leave this principle for last because I believe that you know yourself better at this point than you did on page one. Now that you know yourself better, what is it time to boldly swing out and do?

James Dean, the American motion picture actor and symbol of rebellion says, "*Dream as though you would live forever... live as you though you would die today.*"

Where have you been holding back? Where has your body wanted to step in while your mind/head was telling you all sorts of reasons not to?

After working with hundreds of entrepreneurs over the years, I believe we *think* too much! We do not listen to our intuition; we listen to the voice in our heads that tells us we *shouldn't* because "What will they think?' or *can't* because "That's not how it's done" or some similar message that makes us act mildly. We play these messages over and over and over, making ourselves and those close to us crazy. It is time to get out of our heads and into our hearts – listen and boldly act! For the sake of our vision we must act.

I actually believe that if we have a vision that can impact the world in a positive way, it is our *responsibility* to act boldly. Our world needs bold action these days; bold actions from the place of compassion and kindness, love and peace.

My first business coach asked me, once, when was I going to "stand on the mountain and tell the world about my work?" His message was loud and clear: I was marketing mildly, and it was time for bold action! When I started bold action in my business, I had drastic results – a full practice in eight months!

The most frustrated people I know are not in action. And that, in my mind, is the most difficult and depressing place to be. Big Fish take action. They may fail in the process but, in that experience, I guarantee you that they find the learning, they find the perfection. Even failure transforms into stepping stones to greater success.

Action creates failure and action creates success. Both are a part of a successful business and a part of life. The more action, the more failures – and the more successes. We cannot go forward *expecting* to fail, but we can go forward expecting to learn. This is a small shift that has drastic and different results.

Jack Canfield, in *The Success Principles*, calls it "failing forward." To me, no failure is a failure as long as we learn from it and move forward.

What some entrepreneurs do when they fail is to say, "I will never do that again" or "I will never speak to him again." This attitude and perspective makes our world smaller; it excludes rather than letting it expand. It is when we make our world smaller from the experience and focus on it and never try it again that it becomes a true failure.

Big Fish *recover* from failure more quickly than most people because they know the power of where they are putting their energy. If we focus on the failure, guess what? We get more failure. If we focus on the learning from the failure, we change course and move on. This concept of recovering is an interesting one.

Great athletes recover quickly. Watch slalom skiers come down the mountain. When they catch an edge and get off course, they immediately get back in the rhythm and on track. It is when they do not recover from the mistake that they do not finish.

Let us imagine two entrepreneurs who both experienced a failure. One picked himself up, brushed himself off – found the learning and moved forward. The other moped about the failure for a week. Which entrepreneur would you want to work with? Recovering and getting back to our grounded, confident place quickly is critical when it comes to success and boldly acting.

In order to do this, we need to know what gets us back on track. For some, it is meditation; for others, it is a great work out, taking time off, or cleaning up and organizing.

No matter what it is, it is critical that you know it BEFORE you get off track. Then, when you are off track, you can promptly do whatever it takes to get yourself quickly and efficiently back on track. When we do this consistently, we move consistently toward our vision.

What is key here, however, is *getting back* to the *attitude of choice* when we get off course. In other words, when we get off course, do we let it affect our attitude in a negative way? Or a positive way? There is a sequence here that cannot be ignored.

Big Fish first choose their attitude. Second, Big Fish choose the action. Finally, they boldly act. If that bold action results in a failure, they learn from it and take themselves back to the original attitude that they chose.

There is a sense of commitment to that attitude in service of the vision. This is a critical point in being a Big Fish. Big Fish have a *commitment to an attitude.* Big Fish are committed to an attitude because they know that attitude is the path to the vision. As soon as we let go of the attitude and allow our energy to be transferred to a lesser attitude, it affects our actions – we no longer boldly act in a way that will move us forward.

Let's be clear about what I am not saying: I am <u>not</u> saying to ignore the pain, the embarrassment, the loss or the failure. Stop, feel it, be with it for the sake of the learning and the experience. From this place, you can have much more success because now you are including the experience in your life, not excluding it. What you can be with now is more, not less.

A Big Fish named Tom is an accountant by trade but truly an entrepreneur at heart. He is in his second or third business, is successful and works hard. Talking with him the other day, I could hear a sense of freedom in his voice. He proceeded to tell me he had made the decision to leave his business after being deeply frustrated for a few years. He was no longer having fun like he wanted to. He was no longer having the success he wanted. It was time for bold action. That bold action set him free! He was giggling and giddy. He had been pondering this for a long time but was always able to find the rational reason why he couldn't boldly act. Now, he was eager and excited about his life and the new business opportunities that he used to only dream about.

Sometimes in order to experience the world more fully, we need to let go. I like the analogy of "traveling light." In order to see the world, it is easier to move about with fewer luggage bags. Less "stuff" to take with us – and while "stuff" can literally be material possessions, it is also the heavy thoughts that we make up and carry around each day in our minds. It can be a heavy relationship, personal or professional, that does not allow us a feeling of freedom. It can also come from taking on responsibility that is NOT ours to take on. When we take responsibility for others and do not allow them to take their own, we are robbing them of their own learning opportunity. It can also be a worry about something that has not yet happened but we fear might. All this is 'stuff' that weighs us down.

"Stuff" can be almost anything that makes us feel heavy. An amazing phenomenon that I have noticed in working with Big Fish is sometimes when we begin to let go of stuff that makes us feel heavy, we actually lose weight, too! I have seen this happen consistently among many Big Fish. They are not sure how it happens so easily, but it happens! This is where the mind and body are so tightly woven and directly connected to one another. Bold action has results that affect us all in very different ways.

In some cases, the bold act is sticking it out; in others, it is letting go. Only you know which one is the right bold action for you. The place to look for that answer is not in your head but in your heart. What does your intuition say? What does your biggest vision of all point you toward? I like to ask Big Fish, "What is the action that has you momentarily hold your breath, and gets you all excited inside if you think about doing it?" THAT IS THE BOLD ACTION YOU ARE LOOKING FOR!

There is a beautiful quote by Elisabeth Kubler-Ross: *"How do geese know when to fly to the sun? Who tells them the seasons? How do we, humans, know when it is time to move on? As with migrant birds, so surely with us, there is voice within, if only we would listen to it, that tells us so certainly when to go forth into the unknown."*

Think about throwing pebbles in water – those small pebbles have an impact. Then think about throwing a large rock in water – that action has much bigger impact, a larger splash. My challenge is to boldly act; bold actions have bigger impact. Consistent bold actions actually allow us to do more in less time, therefore bold actions allow us to take more time off over the course of our worklife. What bold action could you take that would have a big impact on your business?

Many entrepreneurs say they do not have enough time off or they feel guilty if they take time off. Guilt is the number one reason we do not live fully. It is the number one reason we do not make change. And guilt is the most useless emotion we can feel. It encourages more of the same behavior; because we feel guilty, we punish ourselves by doing more of the same lousy behavior!

If anything makes you feeling guilty, ask yourself: "What am I getting from punishing myself? And what will break this cycle and encourage me to take excellent care of myself?" You see, if we take better care of ourselves it gives others permission to do the same. When one person feels less guilty, it has a domino effect on all those around him! It is your responsibly to break the habit of feeling guilty. It makes you live small. Guilt is also a red flag, screaming for you to change the aspect of your life that you are feeling guilty about. Address it immediately!

Wild success is possible with wild, bold actions. But our brain does not want us to see them; it is afraid of us seeing them. It is our intuition that first sees those bold actions. Often times we tend to strategize our actions based on our thinking. This is normal and good planning. However, being a Big Fish means doing more listening to our intuition and less thinking. For example, a Big Fish was doing well in her business; she had a consulting practice and it was doing well. She, however, had a larger vision for it. It was against the bottom line in her checkbook to spend more money on marketing, PR, advertising and support because she really could not afford to bring on all those experts, but her instincts said that was the perfect time to do so. She went ahead and used money from her savings account to fund her venture, and that bold action took her business to a whole new level that she would not have been able to do without diving in financially. Her checking account told her not to, but her instincts knew that this was the perfect next step. Instead of being bound by fear, she followed her instinct that knew what was possible.

Actions we take based on emotion are typically very different actions from those based on our intuition. Our intuition tends to have us do things that do not seem natural. For example, in order to get more done, our emotions will tell us that we need to speed up; our intuition will know that we need to slow down.

So many times in life and business, we make decisions from a place of anger and guilt and frustration, and those actions create more of the same in our lives. When we are in the place where emotion is ruling us, it is critical to stop ourselves. Breathe and reground. This can take moments or it can take months! The key here is to notice that we are acting on emotion. We must once again find that place in ourselves that is grounded, and then we can listen more clearly to our intuition. From here, we make choices that are based on vision and our heart's desires and are, generally, decisions that we can feel good about even if they are hard decisions. They create wild change in our businesses and lives.

Bold actions create more time! Bold actions allow us to take more time off because bold actions allow us to accomplish more, make more money and hire more people. Here is another way to look at the old adage, "It takes money to make money": When we are in a place of "not enough money," we need to spend more to change the flow of how money is coming in. PLAY WITH THIS. To me, one of the biggest benefits of running our own company is that we can take time for ourselves when we want. For example, I love to ski or kayak on a weekday when the lakes and mountains are quiet. We get to enjoy life in our rhythm, not the rhythm of the world. And the way we get to do more of this is to create bold actions!

Thinking about this principle reminds me of my trip to Puerto Rico not so long ago. At the resort where I was staying, there was an infinity pool. I had never seen one of these. The pool is built on a cliff, and when you are sitting poolside, you see the water at the far side gently going over the edge and appearing to fall off into the Caribbean about 500 feet below. The two different blues merge at the edge of the pool. I was intrigued and quickly got myself to the edge to see what was over there – and found that the edge was not the edge! It *appeared* to be the edge from one perspective, but the side of the pool actually continued down the mountain. This was a wonderful learning: The edge only appears to be the edge a lot of the time; when we get close to it, there is a whole new edge! The bold act is going to your current edge. You can decide if that is enough or if you want to go further, but without going to the edge, you are not stretching. You get to decide if stretching is a value that you want to honor. If so, how often? I consciously try to find an edge of some sort each day. To me, that is what fully living is all about.

It is important to note that bold acts should also be authentically our own bold acts. What this means is that our actions need to be in alignment with who we truly are. If we try to take bold actions that are not truly us, we find that we cannot follow through on the bold act. For authentic bold action, it is critical that we follow our heart.

A Big Fish named Craig, who had been involved in a large family business and had turned to doing coaching and consulting work, had been standing on the edge of his life looking out. One day, he decided he was ready for bold action. I remember our phone conversation, and the tone in his voice shifting dramatically from hesitation to "I am going for it!" Since that day, he has not looked back and he has not stopped taking bold actions, in both his business and his life, and he is more alive because of it. The Big Fish process is supporting him to continue to boldly act.

My sense is that he is having more impact in his work, he is more fun to be around at home and he is enjoying his life more, too! His bold act was to buy a franchise, run for office, and actively seek a large sponsorship for the sake of growing his business. He now owns a franchise, holds that public office, and has multiple streams of income. It is just as he wrote in his vision, but it is coming true much sooner than he planned. He is moving rapidly toward his vision; it is calling him forth to do so. No one is standing over him to motivate him. He is purely self-motivated – as Big Fish always are.

Bold actions look different to each of us. Someone else's bold actions may not look like bold actions to you. It is not up to us to judge another's bold action. It *is* up to us to consistently inspire our own bold actions. Just to give some examples, the following are some of my bold acts:

When I was laid off from my first job out of college, I chose to start my own business rather than get a job. Being laid off was the kick I needed to do it. If I had not been laid off, I would probably still be playing it safe as an employee rather than stepping into my passion at the time.

My former husband and I had our own business. About a year in to the business, we applied for a rather large bank loan. The bank turned us down. At that moment we looked at each other and without words, knew what the bold action was: to fund the business ourselves. We were committed to our vision, no matter what, no matter who said 'no' for whatever reason. We were determined to grow the company; we had a vision, and no one was going to stop us. We were creative and we grew that business without the bank loan.

Another bold act was leaving a three-year corporate contract that was not only not fun but also made me feel out of integrity with myself. I left without a plan of what I was going to do next.

Writing this book was a bold act. I never saw myself as a writer; an inspirer, yes, but not a writer. I was with an old friend who was not seeing how he was fully responsible for his life. I knew that I had a message, I had information and words of advice and much to say about the importance of creating a life and business that are wildly successful. It was almost out of frustration of listening to this old friend, where I could see his potential and he could not. It was that frustration that inspired me to sit down that weekend and start writing.

I also remember as kid, wanting to fly like a bird with the wind on my face. Years later, I had the opportunity to hang glide off the coast of San Francisco. Of course, I took the leap – and that was the day I decided that every day of my life I needed to take some sort of bold action or leap. That has made all the difference.

In business terms, the bottom line regarding this principle is to plan the work, work the plan, and then go for it! But don't act just to act or react. Take wise action that fits your vision, plan and strategy, and resist the urge to "throw spaghetti against the wall."

William Joseph Slim said it best when he said, "*When you cannot make up your mind which of two evenly balanced courses of action you should take - choose the bolder.*"

Practical Tips and a Writing Exercise:

What attitude do you choose for the sake of your vision?

Name 3 things you want to BOLDLY ACT on today.

1. ____

2. ____

3. ____

Name 3 things you want to BOLDLY ACT on this week.

1. ____

2. ____

3. ____

Name 3 things you want to BOLDLY ACT on this month.

1. ____

2. ____

3. ____

Name 3 things you want to BOLDLY ACT on this quarter.

1. ____

2. ____

3. ____

Name 3 things you want to BOLDLY ACT on this year.

1. ____

2. ____

3. ____

Name 3 things you want to BOLDLY ACT on every day.

1. ____

2. ____

3. ____

Put these BOLD actions in your to-do list.

"*Only those who will risk going too far can possibly find out how far one can go.*" - T.S. Eliot

Being A Big Fish for Life

When we pull the 7 Big Fish principles together, we begin to live a life that has meaning, is in motion and is full of compassion, all at the same time. These principles, when lived consistently, are the foundation of becoming a Big Fish. You see, being a Big Fish is about living fully today from our vision of tomorrow. It is rather simple yet very different from how our world functions today, which is to live from yesterday or a moment ago. Big Fish live large in this moment with tomorrow as the guide.

Big Fish give energy to that which they want to grow. They have a vision that calls them forth daily. They are fully responsible for that vision and trust that the universe will guide the way as well – all the while loving the present moment. Big Fish stand firm and do not let the waves throw them completely off course. They learn from the bumpy waters along the way, and stand firm in who they are and where they are going. They are kind before trying to prove themselves right, in service of the bigger picture of where they are headed in the world. Big Fish trust in the perfection of the world just as it is and work with it rather than fight it. Because Big Fish are making decisions from their instincts and hearts, they boldly act! These bold actions have great impact.

Any time a Big Fish gets off course, there is one magic question to get back on track:

What is my vision calling for right now?

And if we answer that question *honestly and authentically* no matter where we are, we will be pointed in the right direction to reach our goal.

It is critical to keep sight of our vision and our goals. Big Fish take a lot of time over the course of each year to plan, to retreat and to go within themselves to get clear on their visions and goals.

Steven Covey, founder of the Seven Habits of Highly Effective People, will tell us that we do not spend enough time planning. I absolutely agree with him. My challenge to all Big Fish is to take off *at least* two days per quarter just to plan and update your vision and the goals to get there, to ensure that you are on track and moving toward where you want to go. This is more than a full week each year just to maintain, clarify and update your vision! It is critical work if we are committed to our visions. Visions change over time and, therefore, our actions need to be adjusted accordingly.

Anytime a Big Fish does not feel in touch with their vision, it is a message to *retreat,* to go within. Going within might look like shutting the office door, going for a walk or a run, going away alone for a few days, going to the library and not bringing your cell phone. Whatever it looks like – do it and *do it immediately*.

When we feel most lost is when we need to stop moving. We must do this deliberately, because our tendency when fear kicks in is to move faster – emotion driving us instead of intuition. But if we stop and listen to our instincts, we find our way back out of the darkness and the fear.

"*Retreats are deliberately conceived opportunities to back off from the chase, attend to personal inventory-taking, and then go deeper---exploring what you normally neglect, getting better acquainted with whatever in you needs to be forgiven, nurtured or germinated... A retreat is a refuge from a world in which you may have lost yourself and a place where you can find yourself.*" - John R. O'Neil, quoted from *The Paradox of Success*

Once we have our vision again, we are back! We are on track and we can once again make decisions from the end in mind.

Being a Big Fish is not always easy. But it also is not hard. What this means is that it takes us standing firm in our hearts. When we do this, sometimes others get hurt – not because we want them to, but because we are not doing what they want us to do. It is never a Big Fish's intention to hurt another. It is, however, a Big Fish's intention to take care of themselves in service of their visions they are creating each day. You see, Big Fish, take care of themselves in service of having others take care of themselves. Many get stuck in this place and see it as selfish, or feel guilty because they are taking care of themselves. The Big Fish perspective is that doing this is responsible! We have all have heard the following:

"*If you give a man a fish, he will have a single meal. If you teach him how to fish, he will eat all his life.*" - Kwan Tzu

I like to think that "fish," in this case, means happiness, success and bliss. If you help make someone happy for an instant, they have one experience. If you teach them how to make themselves happy and successful, they are happy and successful for life. I actually see the first as more selfish! In that case, we make someone else's happiness depend on us! Talk about letting our egos get in the way!

This does not mean that Big Fish do not lend a hand or offer help! Big Fish often help others! Real Big Fish help others to stand like a rock in who they are for their own happiness and their own success. It is a Big Fish's responsibility to take care of themselves so that others can also take care of themselves. When people take good care of themselves, we have a healthier and more peaceful office, we have a healthier and more peaceful home and we have a healthier and more peaceful planet.

We see another example of this in a school of fish. Each fish, swimming on its own, is fully responsible for himself or herself. And together it is easier to swim because they are swimming as a school, moving with the current that they are all creating together. But the fish first must swim alone, independently of each other. Like them, we must take care of ourselves and ask for what we need. Big Fish sometimes swim with the school and sometimes do not. Big Fish are always pointing others toward what those others need more of. Big Fish are always aware of whether or not their actions are moving them toward their vision.

To summarize, if you are going to be in the business/entrepreneur game for the long haul, from time to time you need to give your mind, body and spirit time to regenerate. Retreat to a favorite thinking spot, take a weekend vacation alone or just make sure you get in that run or yoga session. Better ideas, more focused energy and more balanced success will follow.

When Big Fish follow these principles consistently, they transform their lives and businesses to be wildly successful, outrageously fun and much more balanced. They hear laughter more, they enjoy moments more, they have a strong sense of purpose. They understand what their life is for and live it fully. From here, BIG FISH FLY! They transform into birds and soar!

A request:

We want to hear your stories!

How are the Big Fish Principles changing your world?
How is your business better?
How is your life more fulfilled?

Please, share your Big Fish stories with us via email at
stories@bigfishnation.com

BIG FISH THEME SONG.

If You Can't Fly © 1993 David Roth & Chuck Pyle

www.davidrothmusic.com ~ www.chuckpyle.com

Two old birds in the sun, gray and weary
Neither moving to the pond, far away
It's too hot out here today
Finally one lifts a wing, but the other says "Too tired,
I'll just sit where I am, it's too difficult to fly
Don't think I can"

"Come along," says the first,
"If you want to quench your thirst
You've got to move, shift around
Put your beak into the ground
Bit by bit, closer still, it's just a matter of the will
Side by side, step by step
Come ride the wind up to the water and get wet

And If you can't fly you can run, if you can't run you can walk
If you can't walk you can crawl, that's the beauty of it all
If you can't crawl you can roll, keep your eyes upon your goal
You have your place in the flock, if you can't roll
Then you can rock

Two old fish, slow and cool, reminiscing in the pool
About the times they got away and their friends who didn't
Pay attention, don't get hooked, ride the center of the stream
Go with the flow until you know
And you can swim right up the river to your dream

If you can't swim, you can row, if you can't row you can glide
If you can't glide you can ride, that's the beauty of the tide
If you can't ride you can roll, keep your eyes upon your goal
You have your place in the boat, if you can't roll
Then you can float

Who said you couldn't do it
Who dug you in that hole
You'll only see your obstacles
Each time you take your eyes off of your goal

Two old friends sitting round, sometimes birds and sometimes fishes
Sometimes running all aground in the gaggles of big wishes
Belly-flopping on the pond, stumbly wobbling on and on
But take a step every day and pretty soon
You'll climb that mountain in your way

And If you can't fly you can run, if you can't run you can walk
If you can't walk you can crawl, that's the beauty of it all
If you can't crawl you can roll, keep your eyes upon your goal
You have your place in the flock, if you can't roll

Then you can rock.

The Vision of Big Fish Nation

The vision of Big Fish Nation is for entrepreneurs and corporate teams go through a year-long program implementing the principles in this book via teleclasses and professional coaching. They will work smarter, not harder. They will have more fun and make more money. They will implement their plans in year one and follow them for the next 10 or 20 years.

Within six months of joining the program, Big Fish have a vision for themselves and their business, and that vision is backed by a written plan. They participate in Big Fish events after year one in order to maintain and clarify the vision.

Each year, we travel together to set goals and gain clarity for our individual visions and businesses. Also annually, we take a trip to an underprivileged part of the world either locally or not and we inspire others to have a vision and go for it, while at the same time we are still working in our successful sustainable businesses. We utilize a national media partner to help share our Big Fish stories. As people grow and change and step into their Big Fish life, we want to highlight their stories nationally for the sake of inspiring others to go for it, too.

Big Fish know other Big Fish all over the world. Big Fish are of like mind, and support each other. Big Fish Nation is a community of folks who are making a difference in their own lives and in the world today. Wanna be a Big Fish?

www.bigfishnation.com

Participating in the Big Fish Nation Program

If, after reading this book, you would like to learn more about the Big Fish Nation program and about developing a deeper understanding of the principles in this book, living them fully and having that Big Fish network for the rest of your life, call us today. We will be happy to speak with you about the program.

info@bigfishnation.com

If you would like to be on our Big Fish email list for "Big Fish Food" – email newsletter@bigfishnation.com and let us know you would like to be added to our mailing list and what email address you would like us to use, and we will be happy to add you to our mailing list.

Acknowledgements

Thank you, Robin, my sister, for speaking your truth to me always. You are a very Big Fish in the world, having huge impact on your industry. I am very proud of you.

Thank you, Grandma B., for being a sounding board and showing me what unconditional love truly is. You are amazing.

Thank you, Grandma N., for allowing me to care for you during your final months with us. It was the greatest gift you could have ever given me. I live more now and you live more with me now, too.

Thank you, L.A., for holding me so big consistently. I am grateful you have been my coach for so many years. I finally get it that Big Fish have no hands because there is nothing to hold onto – just let go, swim and love life from there; abundance is everywhere.

Thank you, Kimberly, for your editing, your words of wisdom, your support and most of all, your friendship for most of our lives. You constantly inspire, open doors and ground me. You are a gem and a Big Fish in my life.

Thank you, Kathy, for being my cheerleader through this process of writing. You made all the difference. Your listening, your eagerness, your reminding me who we each are in this world has been a consistent reminder for me.

You have given my feet wings and for that I am forever grateful.

Thank you, Gail, for holding me as a Big Fish when I wasn't, at critical times in my life. It made all the difference.

To each of the Big Fish (and clients): You inspire me every single day, more than you know. You consistently strive to grow, reach higher and move toward your goals. It is truly an honor to work with you. You are proof that Fish Fly!

The following friends and family have inspired me to either complete this book or write parts of it. Thank you for being you and being in my life: Joey, Jodie, Rob, Jim, Hope, Kathy, Larry, Dave, Samy, Michael, Bob, and Lloyd.

Thank you, Wayne Dyer, for being a mentor and role model for me over the past twenty-and-then-some years!

About the Author

Lorin Beller is the founder of Big Fish Nation a unique, year long development program that helps entrepreneurs define, capture and execute against their unique business and life vision.

Lorin's commitment to bringing together the worlds of the mind, body and spirit comes from a combination of formal education, personal passion and real-world business experience.

She holds a biology and psychology undergraduate degree, a masters in Health Administration and is also a Professional Certified Coach (PCC) through the International Coaches Federation.

She began down her career path as a stress management and goal setting trainer, counselor and entrepreneur in the wellness/health industry. She then went on to co-found, develop and sell Global 2000, a technology company. Following the sale of that company, she continued with the publicly-held acquiring company BiznessOnline as the VP of sales and marketing and was a key player in helping the organization acquire and integrate over 13 businesses in a 2.5 year time span.

After this period of tremendous growth and learning, Lorin left the corporate world to follow her next dream... coaching fellow-entrepreneurs in a new way of approaching business, life, change and success. In January

2004, Lorin launched Big Fish Nation and now, helps groups of entrepreneurs from across the country make a "big splash" with their lives and their businesses.

Lorin's ground breaking work has been recognized by leading national business publications including *Investor's Business Daily* and *Female Entrepreneur Magazine* who named her one of the Top 30 Female Executives in 2004. She was also named Entrepreneur of the Year for 2005 by the Guilderland, NY Chamber of Commerce.

Lorin has been a featured speaker at local business and health venues as well as at Sales & Marketing Executives International (SMEI) and the Young Entrepreneurs Organization (YEO). She, and some of the Big Fish, have also shared the Big Fish approach with listeners of the Kathryn Zox Radio Show and Frankie Boyer Radio Show.

Lorin is a member of the National Association for Female Executives (NAFE) and serves on the Boards of the Guilderland, NY Chamber of Commerce, Guilderland Economic Development Advisory Council and the Sales & Marketing Executives of Upstate New York.

Lorin currently lives in upstate NY with her protégé, Niki, a Sheba Inu (about 20 pounds!).

Ralph Waldo Emerson says,
"Live in the Sunshine, Swim the sea, Drink the wild air."

Printed in the United States
32222LVS00002B/124-237

9 780976 955801